DUFOUR EDITIONS
Booksellers and Publishers
CHESTER SPRINGS, PENNA.

EUGEN KUSCH · MEXICO

MEXICO
IN PICTURES

With Photographs and Text

by

EUGEN KUSCH

HANS CARL · NÜRNBERG

The dust cover shows parts of the mosaics of the Teatro Insurgentes, Mexico City,
by Diego Rivera, 1955

The cover has the picture of the Aztec god of rain, planting a tree, and the god of death,
pulling it out again. According to the Codex Tro-Cortesiano, Madrid

The illustration on the foly-leaves is a reproduction of a wall-painting in the tomb 105
in Monte Albán, Oaxaca, showing Zapotec deities at a procession

Second revised edition.
Photographs and text are copyright by Hans Carl, Nürnberg, 1957.
Printed in Germany 1963/65

Cover design by Toni Burghart, Nürnberg.

Printed on paper by Scheufelen K.G., Oberlenningen.

Stereo by Reinhardt & Co., Nürnberg. Printed by J. G. Weiss, München

Life in a southern Mexican village. According to a painting in the ‚Temple of Warriors' in Chichén Itzá, Yucatán

INTRODUCTION

The Federal Republic of Mexico which nowadays includes 31 states and territories of varied climatic, ethnographical and linguistic characteristics in peaceful coexistence is not a country in the sense of the word used by a European but rather a continent, indeed almost a world in its own right through its wealth of vastly different soils, flora, fauna and folklore. Its amazing variety of landscapes, its many places where eternal spring meets vast snowy regions, its original Indian culture, its pagan relics testifying to a great heroic history, all these charm an ever-increasing number of visitors from all over the world. Others may be attracted by its great natural resources. There is hardly a mineral which cannot be mined from its soil. Silver takes the first place among them; then there are iridescent opals and deep purple amethysts of remarkable beauty. More important, however, in the modern struggle for existence, are crude oil, iron-ore, coal, copper and lead, which guarantee Mexico's increasing political and economical scope.

All this flows from a gigantic cornucopia whose narrowest and most curved part is formed by the Isthmus of Tehuantepéc, washed by two oceans, which extends from the U.S.A. in the north to Guatemala-Honduras in the south, a length of almost 3000 kilometres. This corresponds in length to the distance between Lappland and Sicily and in breadth to that from the South of France to Senegal. We have only to glance at its history and social structure and the density of the population to know that the ‚Estados Unidos Mexicanos' have not enjoyed independence for long. About 30,000,000 people inhabit an area of 1,970,000 square kilometres i. e. about 15 people per square kilometre. This is even more astonishing if we remember that more than 4 million people

5

live in the metropolis and even the most remote hamlets seem to be rapidly and steadily increasing in size. But we must not forget that bordering on the cultivated areas there are vast regions of barren mountain country, the Sierra, which like a spine stretches through the whole continent, grandiose to look at in the blue lines of its majestic sweep but hostile to all attempts at cultivation or cattle grazing.

In this varied and rich world it is easy to pass in a single day from the damp heat of the seashore to the icy air of the glaciers and volcanoes, of which there are more than 120 of a height of 3000 metres in Central Mexico. Indeed it is possible at several places of the *Tierra fria,* the cooler region, say, in December, to experience all four European seasons in one day. The contest between tropical sun and thin air hardly registering warmth creates differences in temperature which can vary as much as 25 degrees Centigrade. Modern means of transport and many excellent roads make it possible for the traveller to breakfast under banana palms on the Pacific coast, perhaps in Manzanillo or Acapulco; to rest after lunch in the mild sunshine of Taxco and to reach the metropolis by the evening – a bit short of breath, perhaps, for the thin mountain air is rendered even more difficult to breathe by the exhaust fumes of thousands of cars. From there you can watch the sunset glow on the mountains round the lake Tezcoco and the southern stars appear in the cold night sky. Those who are even more given to hurry and speed can watch all this pass like a film from the window of their aeroplane and they will also learn that though Mexico City for long only had a modest railway station, it has one of the finest airports in the New World. The railway was never much liked in this country of precipices and mountain-passes, of earthquakes and tropical thunderstorms. The transcontinental coach, which connects the remote provinces in a regular and frequent service, and covers distances of over 1500 kilometres, is much favoured. You can even travel from New York to Mexico City in a comfortable Greyhound bus; a distance of 4000 kilometres. It is therefore not surprising that the progressive Mexicans soon took to aviation and use the aeroplanes for pleasure, business and freight. The native Indian, on the other hand, still travels short and long distances by old-fashioned methods: on foot or horseback, on jolting carts or in worn-out automobiles, penned-up with his family, his pets and belongings. There is hardly another country in the world where you find such a sharp contrast between extreme modernity and addiction to the ways of the past.

Nobody with an eye for the beauty of nature will be able to forget how after a two hours' drive from Mexico City to Cuernavaca in descending from the Pass of Tres Cumbres (3000 metres) the air seems to get milder at every bend of the road, while the fir trees gradually give way to subtropical vegetation. This perpetual alternation between an abundant vegetation in the lower regions, where constant humidity and heat transmit the germ of decay even to the unborn life, and the deadly sterility of the bare mountain areas seems to influence the life of the Mexican: he is used to having everything or nothing according to the inscrutable will of nature and providence and to stand in awe of the powers which impartially provide or destroy.

The Mexican Indian has been formed by this contrast and in spite of centuries of subjugation and repeated attempts to exterminate his race, has held on and seems steadily to gain ground. Not that he is trying to regain political control of the country, for he has learnt to exercise restraint, and, like an animal in the jungle, he is guided by an instinct which makes it impossible for him to endure either transplantation to foreign soil or participation in a way of life that is alien to him. He is neither very good at arithmetic nor at organization, but he is a hard working farmer. Even shrewd tradesmen often have a limited understanding of figures. Once in Taxco after long and obstinate bargaining the Indian woman from whom I wanted to buy some silver ornaments asked me to pay for each item separately as she could not add up the sum. For the same reason farmers ask for one thing only, pay for it, leave the shop, and soon return for the next item on their shopping-list.

Like their country, the Indians as a race are not homogeneous. There are numerous tribes who have nothing to do with each other. Learned opinion differs widely as to the identification of the true races. Jorge A. Vivió distinguishes ten tribes for the whole of America, of whom six live in Mexico. Among these six the most important down to the present day are: the Oaxaquidos, which include the Zapotecs, Mixtecs and Chinantecs, who live in the state of Oaxaca; the Istmidos, whose main representatives are the Mayas, and who inhabit a large area between the Gulf of Tehuantepéc and Panama; the Uto-Aztecs, who live in Mexico and the south-western states of America. In this latter region among the Pueblo Indians may one day be found the legendary ‚seven caves‘ (Chicomoztóc) from where since the tenth century the Nahua tribe emigrated to Central Mexico. Of all these peoples only the Mayas and Aztecs have formed politically and culturally organized states comparable to European countries.

At the time of the Conquest, there were between ninety and a hundred and twenty-five different dialects in Mexico, a third of which have since become extinct. To-day fifty-two Indian languages are still spoken, which make up five main linguistic groups and five subsidiary groups totally unrelated to each other. In addition there are isolated languages, such as the dialects spoken by the Otomís in Central Mexico, the Tarascos round the lake of Patzcuaro, the Mixtecs in Oaxaca, or the Totonacs in Vera Cruz, which again show no affinity with each other. The dialects sometimes differ so much that people from various parts of the country can only with difficulty communicate with each other. More than three and a half million people are subjected to this Babel of tongues, which is nowadays partly overcome by a kind of Spanish interspersed with Aztec words. This, however, is spreading rapidly under the new law of compulsory school attendance.

On the other hand, the unprejudiced observer of the Central American Indian is impressed by a deeper unity which seems to be based on the fundamental similarity of their philosophy of life and suggests a kindred origin. This impression is strengthened by recent research. A great number of identical archeological finds leads to the conclusion that all the Indians of the New World immigrated from a Far Eastern country in pre-historic times, generally put at about fifteen thousand years before our era. All the Indians share a number of strikingly uniform characteristics: a graceful, neat figure, slender build, light-brown skin, mostly round heads and black hair, often sparse in men. Many Indians have an Asiatic look about them which might conjure up associations with Eskimos and Tibetans, Chinese and non-Aryan Indians. A connection with the latter would be a kind of belated justification of the name of Indian, given to the natives by Columbus.

Since the Conquest there has been an increasing but not always fortunate mixture of races, which has given Mexico a new appearance. About fifty-five per cent of the present population are *mestizos* of Spanish-Indian blood. They are chiefly town-dwellers. Customs, native clothes, country festivals, religious and secular buildings, the arts and literature, all reproduce this fascinating amalgamation of two once totally alien civilizations. It is expressed in many small details: the broad-rimmed straw hat, the Spanish sombrero, is worn by the Indians with their traditional clothes of gaily-striped hemp and nobody who looks at the homogeneous effect could believe that the straw hat – like horse and cart – is a gift from the European invaders.

The same is true of the musical instruments of chiefly Spanish origin, the harp, the guitar and the African marimba, or the cut of many women's dresses: they have been assimilated to the Indian's needs and traditions. In a similar fashion in the arts and in literature the two civilizations have been welded into a unity as is so well illustrated in the poetry of Sor Juana Ines de la Cruz when she attempts to show a basic relationship between the Aztec blood sacrifice and the communion cup of the Christian religion.

By many photographs and detailed descriptions this book sets out to give a colourful picture of the Mexican world and as in my book on Egypt I have tried to give a comprehensive survey of the country and to show up many affinities to other civilizations as well as the basic unity which underlies all its creative expressions: Christian art permeated by pagan art, the Spanish patio and other elements of bourgeois culture reconceived and remodelled. This interaction can even be seen in the skyscrapers of Mexico City which though they resemble the huge structures of the U.S.A., yet differ from them in having an element of the old Indian tradition about them. The debt to Indian culture is sometimes slight but in other cases very striking, for instance, in the gigantic mosaic façades of colourful beauty in the modern buildings in Mexico City.

To collect the material for this book I had to travel 20,000 kilometres, almost half the distance round the world. The climate and the geographical situation of the country as well as its overwhelming wealth in folklore, art and history presented me with many difficulties which I could only overcome through the advice and help of many kindhearted people. I would therefore like to express my sincere thanks to the Mexican authorities, who helped me by furnishing me with introductions; to Ignacio Marquona, in charge of excavations at Chichén Itzá, and director of the Instituto Nacional de Antropologia e Historia; to Alberto Ruz-Lhullier, the curator of the temples of Yucatán; and to the Centro de Turismo. Special thanks I owe to all those Mexican and German friends who offered hospitality to me and my wife or took us to places of interest inaccessible by public transport. Lastly, my sincere expression of gratitude goes to the publishing house of Hans Carl, who have encouraged me in every way and have made possible the inclusion in this book of some coloured plates indispensable for the revelation of such a colourful country as Mexico.

RELIGION AND MYTHOLOGY IN ANCIENT MEXICO

In spite of the many alien elements which have influenced Mexico we can still get a comparatively clear picture of Aztec civilization. The Aztec „kingdom" was originally a federation of towns comprising the sister towns of Tenochtitlán-Tlatelolco in the Texcoco lake and parts of the surrounding mainland. It had developed from a tribal democracy to an elective monarchy. The chieftain called himself modestly Tlatoani, speaker in the family council, but also proudly Tlacatecuhtli, lord of the people. He had practically unlimited powers, and the Spaniards therefore gave him the title of emperor. His position can be compared with that of the *pontifex maximus* in Ancient Rome, since he, too, united religious and secular power in his ambitious hands. Originally he had held the position of a chieftain in times of war, and a chancellor of the same social standing was his assistant, called by the title of the goddess Cihuacóatl, chieftain of peace. These two overlords governed with the help of a kind of quadrumvirate, a council of four advisers, who had the status of chieftains. In 1500, when Tenochtitlán had gained the supremacy over Central Mexico, which it tried to extend at the time of the Conquest, this system of government had lost its function and the chieftain had established himself as supreme ruler. The Aztecs had extended their territories to a region of almost the size of the British Isles and exacted tribute from thirty-eight provinces and several smaller states.

Tenochtitlán-Tlatelolco, a kind of Venice situated 2,200 metres above sea level, had according to recent estimates more than half a million inhabitants. Apart from its gigantic temple precincts, it probably did not differ very much from a present-day Indian settlement: a happy cross between a village and a town with unpaved streets, full of turkeys and almost bald Chihuahua dogs, which when fattened are eaten as a speciality. The bigger mansion-like buildings, too, were probably made of adobe, the perishable unburnt brick, and filled with people, the greater part of whom were artisans earning a simple and modest living. The size of such a fast-increasing settlement posed many problems, as did the state itself, which at a period of rapid social development seemed to predict internal crisis as well as further progress.

The inhabitants of Tenochtitlán belonged to a quick and intelligent people who in just over two hundred years managed to adapt themselves to new surroundings and a new way of life and who took passionate possession of their territory after years of forced restraint. The Aztecs resembled the Romans in their feeling for the right political move and their statesmanship, and in their cultural achievements. They appeared at first on the Mexican political scene as the heirs to the Toltecs whom they were clever enough to recognize as their superiors in the realm of art and civilized living. Parallels in European history are easily found: it appears that all higher developed states depend on similar laws like buildings on the laws of statics. In religious matters, however, we have to try and avoid comparisons with European conditions and to remember that each civilization has its own centre, its own religious conceptions, and that therefore its religious manifestations though strange to our feelings are historically justified. The Old Mexicans believed that the whole of the cosmos is older than the sun, that it received life by the creation of the fire and that the sun could only exist through human sacrifice and had to be sustained by them. The dominating religious thought was a profound dualism. As much as one sympathizes with the horror of the Spanish Conquistadores at the sacrificial slaughter of human victims, one has to admit that from a historical point of view it amounted to prejudice, as it so often occurs when two different civilizations meet without preparation. On the battlefields of Otumba and Tenochtitlán the Iron Age met the Bronze Age, or rather the Stone Age, characterized not only by the different materials of which their weapons were fashioned but also by their vastly different level of thought, feeling and worship. Each of the opposing armies went into battle firmly believing in their traditions and the blessing of their gods. But only one could emerge victorious from the battle: the side which best knew how to combine the offensive power of the religious idea with the military power of their hands and was therefore spiritually the stronger. And that, in spite of many shortcomings of the emissaries, was the Christian Spanish side whose power was soon to embrace half the world. Even if the Eagles and Jaguars (American tigers) of Moctezuma's picked troops had succeeded in destroying Cortés' army besieging Tenochtitlán they could not have averted the fall of their empire, only delayed it. - It was reserved for our own century, unprejudiced in metaphysical matters, to develop an almost three-dimensional way of reviewing ancient religions and to show that the dark myth of the Aztecs was not the result of accident but created out of their philosophy of life and the conditions of their native country. These two factors are still at work and have resulted in an interpenetration of Catholicism and paganism which has probably no parallel elsewhere. Besides this there is the fact that all religions develop on fundamentally similar lines and therefore can never be utterly alien to each other. A further factor is the (undoubted) Asiatic inheritance which affects all the peoples in Central America, biologically, psychologically and culturally. This Asiatic deposit is so strong that we must believe that these peoples came originally from the Far East. This link makes it clear that the striking similarity between the pyramids in Chiapas, Yucatán and Guatemala and those of Ankor in Cambodia is no accident. These structures are basically the same as the Zikkurats of Mesopotamia of which the famous tower of Babel was one. It may also be considered a delightful freak of coincidence that the Spaniards erected buildings of this kind in Mexico as we may see from the tapering spiral watch-tower of Los Remedios (fig. 23). Confirmation of this view may be found in the fact that the so-called false vaults of South Mexico (fig. 146) and Guatemala occur in such widely separated countries as Upper India, Crete and Sardinia. In this context it is significant that both the Chinese and the peoples of Central America show a marked preference for fashioning small ornaments in jade. The Mayas and the Aztecs following in their footsteps, however, chose this stone less for its beauty than for its green colour which to them symbolized plant fertility. There are also works of art by the Olmecs, an as yet not identified people who held supremacy long before the Aztecs, which like the pyramid of El Tajín (fig. 60) recall traces of a lost Asiatic civilization.

We also find parallels in religious matters. The Aztecs believed that our earth was the fifth, the last after four previous ones had been destroyed by a terrible disaster, a conception shared by several Eastern peoples and which echoes in the Greek idea of the decline from a Golden to a Bronze Age. In the same way we meet the conception of a multiplicity of heavens and hells in the Chinese and Babylonian religions, from which the Semitic peoples derived many important ideas. The Indians of Central America tell of nine heavens and nine hells, the Aztecs of thirteen which they imagined to be ordered one on top of another like the steps of a pyramid. It is interesting to note that this conception corresponds to Dante's description of the mountain of purgatory except that he speaks of seven circles according to the medieval number of the planets. The pyramid of Tajín (fig. 60), too, tapers to the characteristical platform in seven steps. When Christians imagine hell as situated underneath the earth, or when they speak of being in the seventh heaven, when the original Greek text of the Lord's Prayer begins „Our Father which art in heavens", we are dealing with traces of long forgotten traditions which are distantly related with those of Old Mexico. On the other hand many merely accidental similarities among different civilizations have led to wrong conclusions and it will be a matter for future research to work out the true picture of a difficult relationship.

At the time of the Spanish Conquest the Aztec religion was a demonic kind of polytheism, based on the adoration of many deities, whose individual powers though well defined tended to overlap with each other. The inhabitants of Tenochtitlán like the Romans were eclectics and drew their religion from many sources, above all from the various gods of their conquered neighbours if they seemed particularly useful to them. The deeper reason, however, was

the fact that their religion was not only pre-moral without any good and evil or acknowledging any influence of this world on an after-life, but it was also „a-logic", not a comprehensive system but the result of a number of coincidences which for the individual had become unalterable law. This religion appointed each member his place in the community of the tribe, but it did not offer him any individual solace or any kind of protection in this world or the next. The conception, for example, that everybody who died from natural causes had to wander for four years in a desolate wilderness and was then condemned to dwell in hell for ever was artificially nurtured by the authorities who wanted to encourage the warrior to fight to the bitter end. The warriors slain on the battlefield and people struck by lightning or killed by other disasters were the only ones who could hope for an honourable after-life. The others needed to draw on a fund of resignation to face the melancholy reflections of old age. Absolution, however, could be obtained from some sins, for example, you could do penance before the goddess Tlazolteótl for one act of adultery. This, however, did nothing to diminish the gloom of the after-life of all who did not die on the battlefield.

The religious rites were rooted in a kind of magic, the belief, that nature evolved according to certain laws and could be dominated by an initiated mind and by set phrases. One might perhaps see the precursor of a later natural science in these attempts to recognize the workings of nature. At some time the old Mexican priests may have realized that so far they had been underestimating the natural powers and they elevated them to the same status and furnished them with humanlike features as the gods who had created the cosmos and governed it since the beginning. Such sublime personalities, however, could not be ordered but only adored and prayed to. They acted of their own free and unforeseeable will and one could never be sure that they would grant a wish. This created in the human being the feeling of absolute dependance, as Schleiermacher defines it, without the hopeful note of Christianity with its promise of final salvation. In spite of their belief in a differentiated assembly of gods there was no way to salvation and confessors had to cling to stoicism which rendered them insensible even to the pains of sacrificial death. This resignation is characteristic even of the present-day Indian and has remained unchanged by 400 years of devout Christianity. The Indian loves life but does not fear death. He has a familiar approach to death as to a good friend. The foreign visitor is astonished by the important part the „Calavera" plays in Mexico, the image of the skull which with all other parts of the human skeleton is modelled in bread dough or pastry and eaten on November 1st.

Another step in this enlarged conception of the gods may have been the realization that they could not stand alone, that they, too, had to be in some sort of relationship or opposition to each other like the powers of this world. From these tentative beginnings the Mexicans gradually fashioned the story of creation. There are two beings known to the Aztecs as Tonacatecuhtli and Tonacacihuatl (Lord and Lady of our Flesh) who were represented as the deities dominating the genesis of things by the creation of the male principle of the cosmos in contradistinction to the earth which was thought of as possessing female attributes. There are several legends about the actual creation of the world from the mutilated limbs of a crocodile-like monster Cipactli. We find in them already the idea of self-sacrifice which alone can sustain the planets in their motion. It is interesting that the two creative deities later on ceded some of their powers and the further modelling of the world to other gods, who were far from sublime in some of their actions and more like enormous caricatures of human vice and human weakness, yet totally without the merry charm of the Homeric gods.

This change in the development in a normal nature religion without blood sacrifice was favoured by the needs of the expanding Aztec empire. With the rapid and successful expansion of their kingdom the self-confidence of the rulers grew and they saw themselves as the chosen people of the sun sent to fulfil a divine mission towards their neighbouring tribes. This conception of a special mission soon ran through the whole of private and public life. The warriors attained high social standing. The military spirit, well and methodically fed by the speculations of the priests, soon created a mentality which Alfonso Caso has aptly defined as a „military theocracy". The Spaniards, themselves filled with a sense of mission, met this spirit first in Moctezuma's messengers and immediately saw in it an impiety.

The two creative deities dominated not only the genesis of all things but were also the parents of the four most important astral gods: of the red Tezcatlipoca who also has the names of Xipe and Camaxtli, of the proper black Tezcatlipoca representing night, of Quetzalcóatl and of Huitzilopochtli. Tezcatlipoca and Quetzalcóatl created human beings by drawing their own blood, but they are for ever adversaries, representing an eternal dualism which was already given in the polarity of male and female, and which became one of the fundamental ideas of Mexican religion. The epithet „Ome", two, of the two deities signifies a duality which keeps nature in a perpetual state of tension and inspires all creatures with fear. Our continent is familiar with this dualism from the teachings of Zoroaster and his followers: the conflict between Ormuzd, god of light and good, and Ahriman, god of darkness and evil. But in Parseeism good at last is victorious, while the conflict between Quetzalcóatl and Tezcatlipoca remains forever unsolved, a manifestation of the eternal hopelessness of all life. The drawing from the Codex Tro-Cortesiano on the cover of this book represents this idea: it shows on the left the god of rain, who is planting a tree, while on the right the god of death destroys it.

In spite of the cult of these personified gods, the great mass of the people retained a belief in magic and the workings of impersonal powers in the world which could be invoked by wise men and women. This belief in magic still exists and the priest has to fight a powerful opponent in the village witch-doctor, who has an excellent and ancient knowledge of herbs so abundant in Mexico, and who is thought to be in contact with powers. Even to-day it is the local witch-doctor who adds to the baby's Christian name received in baptism the name of an animal as it was laid down hundreds of years ago in the Tonalámatl, the ritual calendar of the Aztecs. There was also a tendency among the people to exaggerate polytheism, to find the workings of more than one god where the priests saw only one. This tendency has been compared, with due reservations, to the veneration of saints in the Roman Catholic church, which repeatedly added to the number of its saints in the hope of finding assistance in every possible predicament. This purely external similarity has even been quoted as one of the possible reasons why the Indians embraced the Catholic faith so eagerly. They found another link with their former religion in the Christian cross. They had long been familiar with the cross as the symbol of life and had used its arms in a kind of system indicating the different quarters of the heavens. The cross of Palenque, now in the National Museum in Mexico City, belongs to this category. Aztec religion about 1500 was a blend of largely borrowed myths whose origin we cannot unfold, only guess at. One thing is certain, however, this religion led to ever darker views and to greater hopelessness and bondage instead of upwards towards intellectual liberty and ultimate salvation as in other high civilizations. The early Indians offered flowers, maize and incense to their gods, their descendants offered hekatombs of human hearts and yet gained no relief from affliction and inner anxiety. The development was logical in itself: it was believed that the gods by their own example once showed that only renewed offerings of blood would sustain the cosmos. The American ethnologist J. E. Thompson has defined this development as follows: like Ulysses who administered to his dead companions' spirit the blood of the slaughtered animals to revive them, the Aztecs had to feed the sun. During its nocturnal journey through dark gloomy regions it had become a mere skeleton; only when fed with blood does it regain its original strength to take up its daily fight with its brothers, the stars, and its sister, the moon. This process is also described in the legend of the birth of the sun-god, Huitzilopochtli, who, day and night, protects his mother, the earth-goddess Coatlicue, accused of profanation, against the threats of her other children. Like nature the gods, too, become weak and have to be sustained with blood which they had shed, long before the creation of man, to save the world and for which they asked now a return. In Teotihuacán and other temples there was a legend that this or that god had thrown himself into the fire, when, after some cosmic disaster, the sun did not shine any more, in order to rekindle the precious light by this self-sacrifice.

There were several ways of sacrificing the victims and they have often been described with horror. Often the victim was placed on a raised platform and while two assistants held his arms and legs the priest cut open his chest with a flint or obsidian stone knife, tore out his heart, offered it to the sun and then placed it in a stone bowl (fig. 20/21). With the conclusion of each calendar period of 52 years a special ceremony in dread of the last day was held. The gods were placated by the slaughter of the human victim, on whose still living breast a fire of wood was kindled by friction, the heart and body being consumed by the flames so lighted. Torches were lit from the sacred fire and carried to rekindle the domestic hearths. Other methods of immolation were flaying, decapitation, burning. There were also mock-battles with uneven weapons, faintly resembling the Roman gladiatorial games but with a ritual background. No sooner was the victim wounded when he was strung up and shot by an arrow. All these ritual sacrifices, as also the burnings of victims after rendering them insensible by giving them a narcotic, the cannibalism of their flesh etc. are neither conscious nor unconscious acts of cruelty. The victim was no longer a simple human being but the protagonist in a ritual drama, symbolizing the god to whose altar he was brought, clad in his attributes. He could be sure of eternal joy after his brutal death. There is a strong element of ritual drama in the Spring sacrifice in honour of Tezcatlipoca. A young man was set apart a year beforehand and adored as the earthly representative of the deity, whose name, garb and attributes he assumed. He received a careful education, led the life of a prince of the blood and was regarded with awe by the entire populace. Before his time was up he was mated to four women of high birth, who accompanied him part of his last journey to the temple of sacrifice upon the sides of which he broke the musical instruments with which he had beguiled the time of his splendid captivity. When he reached the summit he was seized by the highpriest and laid on the stone of sacrifice. There is a certain element of „barbaric beauty" as George C. Vaillant calls it, in this ritual.

The proposition that all higher civilizations ought to bring consolation and inner harmony to their peoples is perhaps too European an idea, though it seems to be confirmed in the higher civilizations known to us, whatever their political fate. It is no accident that India, China and Egypt rate so highly in the opinion of posterity because parallel with the increase in consciousness they show an ever more intimate working together of all the aspirations that make up civilization, a happy cross-fertilization of religion, art and intellectual activity which was taken as a model by countless later generations. The last but powerful representatives of Old Mexico, the Aztecs, showed outstanding gifts for

many-sided creation, an astonishing feeling for form in architecture and sculpture, which expressed in many different ways their dual vision of reality. Not only did they reveal their gifts in the various arts and crafts, there are beginnings of a literature not possessed by any other Old American people, such as hymns to the gods, epic and historical narratives, shrewd and pithy proverbial sayings. What chiefly characterizes all these manifestations is their close observation of natural processes. They were gifted merchants and political planners. Above all these Aztecs were in their way a deeply religious people, for everything they thought and did and made was done with reference to their religion, down to their very pastimes, as for instance, the game of Tlachtli (fig. 144) to which they were passionately devoted. Where, however, they fall short of ultimate greatness can be seen in their alphabet which, though it allowed them to group together objects in general classes, had no means of expressing abstract ideas. The Aztecs had no drama and no reflections of argumentative logic which might be called philosophy. Their fairy-tales, too, lack dramatic interest. They give the impression of an anonymous voice from the people trying painfully and slowly to come to grips with the legends of creation and origin of the tribe without infusing the splendour of magic, which forms so large a part of the charm of the European fairy-tales. As indicated above the Aztecs had preserved a part of the Stone Age with all the good and bad sides of such assiduous perseverance. We meet this spirit still at work everywhere in isolated communities of modern Mexico and it is justified as long as its results are not measured by modern standards. Consequently the Mexicans preserved customs, which lost their value as they developed. Originally the Mexican idea of self-sacrifice was a noble one, for what could a man offer the heavenly powers of greater value than his own being? The first man who offered himself to the gods to be slaughtered on their altars may have seemed in the eyes of his people to be a saint. But the act of self-sacrifice loses some of its force if it is no longer done by free will and in time of emergency but under compulsion and may be enforced at any time. Christianity has symbolized the idea of self-sacrifice by one exceptional act and has therefore gained a moral impetus which carries conviction down to our days. In Mexico the call for self-sacrifice rose so often, that the idea became debased and the conception of the inviolability of human life, if only as means of existence, was lost. The individual sunk to the level of the sacrificial animal, whose blood had pleased the gods long before they asked for human victims.

When, in 1487, the enlargement of the temple of Huitzilopochtli in Tenochtitlán was finished 20,000 prisoners were offered to the god of war, who had helped in the splendid success of the Aztec empire, at a ceremony of re-consecration. They were all men taken prisoners in the battles with the neighbouring tribes and the skilled priests took four days to slaughter them all. This ritual wallowing in blood has probably no parallels in history and is the more horrible as it could be repeated ad libitum at the order of the priests. The whole of public life was dominated by these immense sacrificial orgies which in reality form a great contrast to the otherwise very gentle mind of the Indians, who love flowers and animals and who were terrified by the tortures inflicted by the Spaniards.

The Aztec warriors had to be careful not to kill their enemies but to make prisoners — sometimes by long honourable discourses — as future offerings to the gods. The military career of a soldier depended on the number of prisoners he could take. When this method of providing human victims failed to supply the required numbers, the Aztecs forced their neighbours to take part in mock-battles, the so-called „wars of the flowers" with the sole object of providing victims for ritual slaughter. The priests saw in a series of unusual occurrences in nature that the country was doomed and they managed to persuade the fanatic but weak Moctezuma, a member of their own cast, that the gods were thirsty and measures must be taken if the catastrophe had to be avoided. The blood of the sacrificial victims went on flowing on the altar stones till the Spaniards put a sudden end to it. It is no mere surmise that the tribes of Old Mexico were decimating each other to an extent which endangered their very existence, as it was almost always the best, who either forcibly or by their own free will, mounted the steps to the temples to secure the duration of heaven and earth.

To refute human objections against this practice, parallels with Roman gladiatorial games have repeatedly been drawn, which though without a religious background were not worthy of a great civilization. The European religious wars, the inquisitions and witch-trials which were even bloodier than the Aztec sacrifices, have also been mentioned in this connection. But these are no justification of these dark cults, quite apart from the moral condemnation which may vary with the individual, with the historical period and with the different types of civilization. Ultimately it is the equilibrium of a nation which gives the individual a peaceful life and that happy sense of security which the Romans expressed by the word „patria". This equilibrium had been upset in the Aztec state long before the Conquest, so that their varied civilization in comparison with other high cultures seems perverted and on the wrong path in the intellectual field which after all gives each nation its particular stamp. It is worth mentioning that some people in Old Mexico recognized this long before the downfall of their country. Netzahualcóyotl, king of Texcoco (1418—1472) for instance, the „fasting Coyote", has often been called the Mexican Solomon by later historians. The king wrote hymns, but is best known for his wise and enlightened rule and the code of laws he framed. His impartial advice was even occasionally sought by neighbouring chieftains. He had

a wide knowledge of astronomy and established an academy of music which served arts and science alike, the purpose of which was to supervise artistic endeavour of every description. He erected large public buildings in Texcoco and Texcotzingo which were all destroyed in 1539 by the order of the first Spanish bishop Juan Zumarraga. The king also erected a temple to the Unknown God, built in the shape of a steep graduated pyramid, its tower covered by a highly ornamented wooden roof like several other temples in the country. In this temple no idols or blood sacrifices were permitted. The god Tloque Nahuaque (Lord of Nearness) accepted only the scent of flowers and the smoke of the copal as the Quiché-Indians in Guatemala light it today before Christian churches. This adoration of gentleness may well be a throwback to a long lost custom. The creative deities, Tonacatecuhtli and Tonacacihuatl, too, did not ask for human sacrifices, nor did Quetzalcóatl who was taunted for this by his opponents. Yet this new conception could not materialize in the wild period of 1500. But these beginnings of a monotheistic peaceful religion show that a king tried to divert his Aztecs from something he had recognized as an aberration — a comforting thought in this gloomy picture of pre-colonial Mexican religion.

In the following pages a short survey will be made of the most important Aztec deities. The less familiar a civilization is for the observer, the more guidance he needs in reviewing its world of thought, ideas and creative achievements. As in Christian art and, indeed, in all religious art mere aesthetic appreciation is not enough in looking at Old Mexican buildings and pictures: this short iconography attempts to further the understanding of the Mexican works of art of the pre-colonial period.

THE MOST IMPORTANT MEXICAN DEITIES

Chac (Rain) is the collective name of the Maya rain-gods, tutelary deities of water and agriculture. They are still worshipped in Yucatán and a kind of mass is celebrated in connection with other farming festivals (misa melpera) and they virtually are still being adored under the name of the corresponding Christian saints.

The sculptures of Ometóchtli, the pulque god, found in Tula (fig. 44) and Chichén Itzá have long been mistaken for the god Chac.

Chalchiuhtlicue (Lady of the Emerald Robe) was known as the wife of the rain-god Tlaloc. She was the goddess of all running water and the humidity necessary for all organic life. This may have been one of the reasons why her name was evoked at the baptism of children to frighten off evil spirits. In the third circle of heaven she reigned over the souls of the drowned but she was also known to live in the mountain of Malinche (fig. 38). She had a blue ornament in her nose and was crowned with a helmet-like coronet of snakes; her robes were decorated with wavy lines and sea-shells. The chief participants in her festivals were fishermen and sailors and all whose occupations brought them into contact with water.

Chantico (the Lady living in the House) is a local goddess of fire, held in special esteem in Xochimilco, and associated with Xiuhtecuhtli. She was the tutelary goddess of the stonemasons and goldsmiths. Her name in the Aztec ritual calendar is „Nine dog" as she had changed into a dog by Ometecuhtli for breach of the fast.

Chicomecóatl (Seven Serpents). Her name derives from the date of her birthday in the Aztec calendar. She lived in the heaven of Tlalocán, the rain-god, and was the tutelary goddess of all food, above all of the maize and she presided also over the fertility of man and the soil. She is represented on the idols with a red-painted face and body and wears a four-sided paper mitra, decorated with rosettes and coloured stripes; her robes have the colour of red spring flowers. Young girls visited her temple in the dark, in festive clothes and with seven maize-cobs in their hands to implore the blessing of the goddess. The cobs were then placed in the home as a fertility magic. Her festivals lasted several days, there was much dancing and offerings of fruits and crops.

Chicunauhápan (the ninefold Stream) was the river thought to be flowing in the West of the Mexican nether-world, which the souls of those who had died an ignominious death from natural causes had to cross on their way to the ninth circle of hell under the guidance of a red dog. It can therefore be compared to the Greek Styx.

Cihuacóatl (Lady of the Serpents) guarded the spirits of the women who had died in child-birth, the large crowd of the so-called Cihuatetéo, who lived in the western part of heaven, in Cincalco (in the House of Maize). On certain days they haunted the crossroads and frightened the travellers at midnight or during the eclipse of the sun. They also afflicted children with epilepsy. The goddess is usually represented with long-flowing hair, her lower jaw bare to the bones. She blessed the sowing of the maize and other agricultural occupations. She also possessed war-like qualities and brought success to the fighting armies. On the whole her appearance was identical with that of Coatlicue and Tlazoltéotl. She is said to have haunted the streets of Tenochtitlan in the garb of a common woman of the people prophecying the imminent destruction of the Aztec empire.

Cintéotl, maize god, son of the goddess Tlazoltéotl, sometimes identified with other fertility deities as, for instance, Macuilxochitl, Xochipilli and the red Tezcatlipoca. He is characterized by a yellow coloured body and face, marked with black stripes which run vertically over his face. He carries maize flowers and corn cobs in his hair.

Cipactonal and Oxomoco, brother and sister, who often appear in connection with the story of creation. The name of the first is derived from Cipactli, whether giant-lizard, toad or sword-fish, the monster from whose limbs the world was formed. Both are known as the inventors of astronomy, divination and the calendric system. Their functions, however, are not very clearly separated from each other.

Coatlícue (Robe of Serpents), the Aztec earth-goddess, supposed to be the mother of sun, moon and stars. She has also given birth in a supernatural way to Huitzilopochtli. Like the earth she was life-giving and life-destroying at the same time, the creative and destructive principle of a merciless love. The Aztecs, in spite of addressing her as „Tonantzin", little mother, have given her a terrifying appearance as can be seen from the colossal statue in the National Museum in Mexico City. The sculpture has two serpents' heads instead of a human face. The serpents touch each other with their long tongues. The hands, too, are serpents' heads. The belt is made of a serpent's skin, a human head dangles from it, from which streams of blood in the shape of snakes are flowing. The necklace on her breast is worked from human hearts and hands; the apron is made of closely interwined serpents and ends in the sharp claws of a tiger. Her breasts hang limp as she had to feed gods like human beings. Just as this idol is not a representative of a possible organic being but is a mere conglomeration of macabre elements, so the goddess it represented was not thought of as a personal power but rather as a force of nature.
Like with many other Mexican deities there was a certain amount of identification between Coatlícue and Tlazoltéotl and Cihualtéotl. Each of them represented a possible image of the earth as the Great Mother who takes back her children when their time is up.

Ehécatl, name of the wind, day in the Aztec calendar. Form of Quetzalcóatl.

Huitzilopochtli (Humming-bird of the South), god of war and the rising sun, was the most powerful among the Aztec deities and tutelary god of their metropolis. He led the Aztecs to leave their legendary native country, the lake island of Aztlan, and after long journeys across the Mexican high plateau, to find a new home on the shores of lake Tezcoco. The Aztecs obeyed his orders and founded a new town on the spot where they had seen an eagle perched on a nopal plant devouring a snake.
There is a myth relating to his origin. After the earthgoddess

14

Coatlícue had given birth to the moon and the stars, she retired to one of the temples and lived there as a priestess in strict abstinence and celibacy. One day she found a feather ball which she liked so much that she placed it in her bosom. But when she looked for it, it had disappeared. At the same time she found she was pregnant. Her children, the moon and the stars, felt this to be a slight on her status as priestess and set out to kill her. But when they were on the point of slaying her, she gave birth to Huitzilopochtli, who saved her and chased away his brothers. He revives this deed every dawn by driving away the celestial bodies and seeing in the new day.

Huitzilopochtli, the god of war, was represented in a cloak of humming-bird feathers, his face painted with blue and yellow stripes or covered with a mask decorated with stars. In his hands he held an Atlatl, a kind of catapult and a bow which he was thought to have invented.

The first temple of Tenochtitlán was consecrated to him and Tlaloc. Each king added something to this temple so that in the end it became the dominating building of the town. Here the practice of propitiating the gods by human sacrifice began. When the downfall of the Mexican empire was prophecied just before the arrival of the Spaniards this practice was vainly extended to monstrous proportions.

Kukulkan (in Yucatán) and *Kúkumatz* (in the high plateau of Guatemala) was the Mayas' literal translation of Quetzalcóatl, green feather-bird. After his introduction by the Toltecs in the South of Mexico he became one of the most revered of the gods.

Macuilxóchitl (Five Flower) was regarded as the patron of all arts. On the whole his qualities are the same as those of Xochipilli, the prince of flowers, and their idols cannot easily be distinguished.

Mayahuél was worshipped as the goddess of the plant Agave Americana which was and still is of great value to the Indians because of its many uses. A kind of paper was made from the fibres of its leaves, which were used for decorating idols in the temple and for making manuscript books. The leaves were used for covering roofs, for ropes and coarser garments; the stem was roasted and eaten; the thorns were made into sewing needles and pins and tools for the ritual bleeding. The most precious produce, however, was the juice of the plant from which the slightly acid, quickly fermenting liquor pulque is still being obtained. All the other parts of the plant came in handy for fires. It is easy to understand that such a universally useful plant was soon identified with a heavenly power and adored as a goddess. Mayahuél was usually depicted as a young woman sitting on an Agave plant. Her head is crowned with coloured feathers, her brow wreathed with a blue ribbon. She carries a bowl of foaming pulque or a rope twisted from Agave fibres. Her husband

was Pátecatl, one of the pulque-gods, the evil symbol of intoxication.

Like the Greco-Oriental Magna Mater, the Cybele of Leptis Magna or the famous Artemis of Ephesos, Mayahuél was pictured with four hundred breasts (a number which means a limitless number in the Aztec language) with which she nursed her four hundred sons, Centzon Totochtin, the gods of drunkenness, usually worshipped under the form of rabbits.

Metztli (Moon), lunar deity, sometimes synonymous with the black Tezcatlipoca. As we can see from the Codex Borgia, the moon is depicted as a sickle-like semi-circle formed of bones. Spots on the moon, which are visible to the naked eye, were turned into a crouching rabbit.

Mictlantecuhtli (Lord of Hades), god of the underworld, the grim and shadowy realm Mictlan, which consisted of nine circles. He lived with his wife in the ninth, in Chicunauhmictlan, in the deepest region of the earth towards the north. All people who had died of an illness and were unfitted to enter paradise had to make a four years' difficult journey before reaching him and when they arrived there was no returning back. The attributes of the Lord of Hades are human bones, a mask in the shape of a skull, which, cut from crystal or chiselled in gold, was worn as a jewel by the priests (fig. 99). When Mictlantecuhtli is represented in full size he wears stars on his dark skin, the insignia of the darkness reigning in his kingdom. Bats, spiders, owls, animals of evil omen, accompany him.

Mixcóatl (Cloud Serpent), Aztec god of the chase and also god of human sacrificial victims. He is thought to have re-erected the fallen skies after the last of the great catastrophes, our great flood. The planet Venus is his attribute.

Ometecuhtli and his wife *Omecihuatl* (Two Lord and Lady) created the gods and thus laid the germ of all life on earth. Immortal and unchanging they existed from the very beginning of the cosmos but they do not seem to have had any influence on its later development. They lived in Omeyocan, the highest of the thirteen heavens, the dual place, where the souls of the children dwell who died before gaining the power of reasoning, and where the souls of men were created and fed with the milky juice of a tree.

The combination of the number two (ome) in the name and dwelling-place of this primal dual deity seems to symbolize the dualism which dominated Aztec religion, that the cosmos is kept in motion by two opposing principles.

No temples were erected, no human sacrifices were offered to these dual deities who did not share the all-too-human passions of the other gods; they were thought of as abstract beings only and probably indicate the beginnings of a monotheistic religion similar to the Tloque Nahuaque of king

Netzáhualcóyotl which were pushed into the background by other conceptions in the steep ascent of the Aztec empire.

Ometóchtli (Two Rabbits) was the chief god of the pulque gods and the drunkenness caused by the tricky nature of the drink. He represents a monotheistic simplification of the four hundred rabbits mentioned in the paragraph on Mayahuél whose names derived from the many tribes of the Mexican high plateau, whose tutelary deities they became.

Pátecatl, husband of the Maguey goddess Mayahuél. Though evil qualities were ascribed to him as he was responsible for debauchery — he was also called the strangler — he was at the same time a god of medicine.

Quetzalcóatl (Plumed Serpent). The name derives from the Quetzal bird, Pharomachrus mocinno. Quetzalcóatl is the brightest figure in the gloomy assembly of Old Mexican gods, the charitable god, the symbol of priestly celibacy and the self-sacrificing spirit, of eternal goodness and wisdom. His life is a shining example of temperance, penance and saintliness. This, however, did not prevent his falling into sin through the wickedness of his opponent Tezcatlipoca. These two gods are in constant strife; their battles symbolize the history of the cosmos.

Quetzalcóatl, more than any other god, loved mankind whom he created by shedding his own blood. He taught them how to till the soil, to measure time, to use a calendar, to prepare the aromatic cocoa and to execute some handicrafts such as weaving coloured materials or cutting precious stones. Above all he gave them maize which the ants had hidden in a hill; then in changing himself into an ant he robbed them of one of the golden corns and took it to man as his staple food.

The appearance and attributes of the god vary according to the qualities attributed to him. When thought of as the chief priest he appears as a wise old bearded man with a white skin. The god doing penance is characterized by the thorn of an Agave and a bone knife, the tools of self-castigation. As god of the winds he wears a pointed hat, a mask with a protruding snout-like mouth and his skin is black like that of his opponent Tezcatlipoca. All round, turned or spiral-like things are consecrated to him in his capacity as god of the whirl-wind. For the same reason the pyramids in his name often have round shape (fig. 56). He also represented the planet Venus though there was an actual god of the morning star, Tlahuizcalpantecuhtli, the Lord of Dawn, to whom the best preserved temple of Tula was dedicated.

Quetzalcóatl not only belongs to mythology but also to historical tradition: he is said to have been the founder of the first Toltec city of Tula (fig. 40/45) which he had to leave suddenly as Tezcatlipoca led him into drink and undermined his self-confidence as just ruler. His journeys to Tlillan Tlappallan, the promised land, led him and his faithful companions through Cholula (fig. 68/69) where he was passionately worshipped, then to the south and to Chichén Itzá and Uxma (figs. 136/50), the Maya territory. On these journeys the legendary person of Quetzalcóatl merged into several other chieftains of his name.

One of the many Mexican legends predicted that Quetzalcóatl would return to his people in a year Ce Acatl (one reed) and initiate a golden age. As the Spaniards under Cortés landed in such a year, in 1519, and their skin was white like that of the Lord of the Plumed Serpent, they were taken as the promised gods, a mistake which helped the amazingly rapid collapse of the Aztec empire.

Tezcatlipoca (Fiery smoking mirror) representation of the night sky, the dark season of the year and of black magic; at the same time inventor of the fire. His often fluctuating appearance reflects the changing of all things in life such as the waning moon, which he represented, too. In addition to this he was thought to know all and hear all, a fact which speaks for his universal importance.

In the dualistic system of the Old Mexican religion Tezcatlipoca is the antagonist of Quetzalcóatl, the white magician, and a representative of evil. According to the myth both opponents were brothers, but hostile to each other from the very beginning. After a time of darkness, before the creation of man, Tezcatlipoca changed into the sun and lit the earth for a period of 678 years, that is for three cycles in the Aztec calendar. Then Quetzalcóatl wanted to be the sun and he hit Tezcatlipoca with a stick so hard that he fell into the sea and was transformed into a tiger. After a lapse of time Tezcatlipoca succeeded in getting the upper hand of his brother. Later on they were reconciled and the other gods made them lords of the firmanent. The track of their common journey across the sky is clearly visible, it is the Milky Way. In a later, historical time, Quetzalcóatl was led into sin by Tezcatlipoca's mirror, the symbol of the deceptive appearance of all things, and he became an exile from his kingdom of Tula (fig. 40/45).

Tezcatlipoca is usually depicted with a black painted body and yellow stripes on the face. His attribute, the fiery mirror, is often attached on his brow, or in the place of one of his legs.

All men of a shady occupation, such as magicians, robbers and other petty criminals payed him a timid homage. But also all those who were afraid of some change in their life, and who in this superstition-ridden community was not, implored his help. At his festival which was supposed to bring about the remission of punishment for all penitent sinners, a young man was sacrificed who as personification of the god had lived the life of a chosen prince under the supervision of the priests.

Tlaloc (the Lord who makes the Earth thrive) god of the rain, lightning and the waters indispensable to all plants,

god of agriculture. Probably because of his vital importance he belongs to the original gods of the Central American peoples. He is Tajín (fig. 60/61) for the Totonacs, Cocijo for the Zapotecs and Chac for the Mayas. His wife or, according to other myths, his sister, was the watergoddess Calchiuhtlicue. He was accompanied by a number of „Tlalocs" representing the various functions of water and having under their dominion lightning, snow, hail and all inland waters. Their dwellingplace was Tlalocán, the heavens on the tops of cloud-covered mountains where all those people went who died by drowning or struck by lightning or of swellings and all who, instead of being cremated, were buried. Tlalocán was thought of as a kind of paradise, a place of plenty and fruitfulness, with magnificent gardens, many rivers and lakes. Here the abundance of water, which so often failed in the season of sowing and planting on the Mexican high plateau, ensured a rich and never failing harvest.

Tlaloc is usually portrayed with a sort of sunglasses — in reality stylised coiled serpents — before his eyes and long tusks which protrude horizontally or turn upwards from his mouth. His clothes are blue like the reflection of the skies in the waters, his face and body dark like the black thundery clouds. The temples of Tlaloc were usually situated in dry regions for which the lifegiving waters were thus implored.

Tlaltecúhtli (Lord of the Earth), personification of the living earth, thought to be a kind of crawling monster with a human head which looked partly like a shark, partly like a lizard. On its skin sat a crowd of scorpions, centipedes and snakes, the emissaries of death. It is the beast Cipactli, which the deities Tezcatlipoca and Quetzalcóatl first created before they transformed it into the originally rough and inhospitable earth. There is also a connection with Cipactonal and Oxomoco in this myth. Like the whole of the Aztec cosmos this creation-myth is full of gloomy signs and wonders.

Tlazoltéotl, sometimes called „mother of the gods", was the personification of sensual pleasures and illicit love, but also tutelary goddess of the medicine-men and witch-doctors. She watched over the process of birth and protected the women in childbirth; her priests cast the baby's nativity according to the calendar Tonalpohúalli. She seduced men to sin but also freed them from the consequences of the evil deed by devouring the „ordure" as her name Tlazolli implies. The penitents came to her idols to confess the sin of immorality and she absolved them. This, however, was only possible once during a life-time and it was on the whole only old men who went to her altar. Above all adulterers went to seek her absolution. She was the only deity of some importance in the moral sphere. The punishments for the sins of the flesh imposed by her priests were fasting, abstention and flagellation.

Her attributes were an ornament shaped like a half-moon on her nose, black paintings round her mouth (the eaten sins)

and distaffs in her hair. In her hand she carried a broom or a rope as symbols of the punishment imposed by her. At her festivals, which were celebrated in spring by large communities and in a strikingly merry way, a woman was immolated. The maize-god Cintéotl was her son.

Tloque Nahuaque (Lord of Immediate Nearness or Lord of All Existence, probably a variant to Ometecuhtli). King Netzáhualcóyotl of Texcoco erected a temple with a nine storey tower and a terrace, richly decorated on the inside with gold and outside with precious stones, in honour of this god. This temple, consecrated to the „invisible god, the creator of all things", contained no idols and the offerings consisted of copal scent and flowers. The king did not forbid the cult of the other deities but he elevated the invisible and indescribable god to the first rank among them.

Tonacatecuhtli and *Tonacacihuatl* (Lord and Lady of our Flesh), synonyms for Ometecuhtli and Omecihuatl.

Tonantzin (Our Honourable Mother) or

Teteoinnan were titles of the earth-goddess Coatlícue.

Tonatiuh was the name of the older sun-god, afterwards superseded by Huitzilopochtli. He had the title of „Lord who spreads Light" and „The precious Child". He was compared in the morning with an eagle flying upwards and in the evening with an eagle gliding downwards, with Cuauhtemoc, whose name was also used by the last of the Aztec rulers.

In his capacity of setting sun, changing at nightfall into the moon, Tonatiuh partially overlaps with Tezcatlipoca.

We find Tonatiuh's impressive picture on the big Aztec calendar stone, where his head forms the centre-piece of the sun-disc (fig. 18 b). Each morning offerings were held up to him and there were festivals in his honour on the days of the eclipse of the sun and especially on the day of „the binding of the years" after a cycle of 52 years, when the counting of the years, months and days started all over again.

Xilonen, who lived ‚like the unripe maize', that is, like a virgin, was depicted as a beautiful richly-dressed maiden. Her functions of watching over the young, still green, maize are partly the same as those of Xochipilli, Chicomecóatl and Cintéotl, the group of deities which personified one or other of the various aspects of the maize plant.

Xipe Totec was the god of Spring, who favoured the sowing of seeds and the growing of the maize plant, the staple food of the Indian. The goldsmiths, too, invoked him as their tutelary god, as did also those with an eye or skin disease. To represent the renewing of life and growth after the winter, the priests attired themselves in a flayed human skin. The name of the god ‚Our Lord the Flayed' derives from this practice. Xipe is usually depicted in the *pinturas* with a crown made of feathers, a cloak of tiger paws and a rattle; he often has a kind of wooden plug between his nose and upper lip and wears a flayed human skin over his shoulders from which blood drops.

Xipe Totec is said to have committed sins like Quetzalcóatl, and to have atoned for the loss of his inner balance by leading the life of a monk. He probably goes back to the Zapotec civilization of Monte Albán, where his picture can often be found.

Xiuhtecuhtli (Lord of the Turquoise, of the Year, or of the Grass) god of fire, was feared as much as loved by the people according to the life-destroying and life-sustaining element he represented. The Aztecs called him among other names ‚Huehuetéotl‘, the Old God, which seems to indicate that he belonged to the earliest deities worshipped by the tribes of Central America. Probably the pyramid of Cuicuilco (Fig. 28) in the neighbourhood of the volcano Xitle was somehow connected with him. He also appears as Touumon in the Teotihuacán, another fact pointing to pre-Aztec times.

Xiuhtecuhtli is characterized by yellow, sometimes bright-red hair, the colour of fire, a headband towards which a turquoise bird is flying, a crown with two feather tufts decorated with scarlet runners or with two pieces of wood for kindling. A stylished red flame often sprang from his mouth. His attribute was the butterfly whose jerky flight was compared with the flickering of fire. He is often the dog who bites or the scorpion who stings like fire.

This ancient god was worshiped in every house and food was offered to him at every mealtime, the hearth being his altar. Here many had statues of the god in a sitting position carrying a bowl on his head for the daily sacrificial fire.

After the lapse of a calendar cycle, every fifty-two years, there was a special festival for the Old God. All fires in the country were extinguished, and only lit again after five days of mourning and fasting by the priests of Cerro de la Estrella to the east of the modern city, who re-kindled it by friction on the breast of a human victim. These festivals usually ended in great joy that the movement of the cosmos was assured again for another sun period.

Xochipilli, the Prince of Flowers, as representative of Spring, belongs to the few Aztec gods who have human features which attract, not horrify. In a limestone sculpture (in the National Museum in Mexico City) he sits with legs crossed, eyes fixed in an upward stare, his arms and legs strewn with flowers. In other representations he can easily be identified by a white butterfly painted on his skin or a stick piercing a heart.

Xochipilli was the protector of love, merriment and leisure, and tutelary god to the fine arts, to dancing, mimicry and *patulli*, the game of dice. He was thought of as the representative of young, untamed life, and brought into connection with the green, succulent maize plant. He lived in the ninth heaven, the eastern paradise, Xochitlicacán; his female counterpart was the goddess Xochiquetzal.

Xochiquetzal (Flower Feather) was the goddess of all flowers and blooms, the mate of Xochipilli, and therefore connected with play and dance, singing and art, and every kind of amusement and pleasure. She helped lovers who got married, but also the courtezans who lived with the bachelor warriors and used to take the field with them.

Her first husband was the rain god, Tlaloc, from whom she was stolen out of paradise by Tezcatlipoca, who made her the goddess of love. In her representations she wears colourful festive clothes and a head-dress of the precious feathers of the Mexican Quetzal bird, and a nose-ring in the shape of a butterfly. She was thought to be the inventor of the art of weaving and sewing. On her chief festival, which lasted for twenty days, a whole Aztec month, women were sacrificed to her, mostly former girl-wives, who submitted voluntarily to their death. After the rainy season little clay idols were buried in the fields as fertility charms. Both Xochiquetzal and Xochipilli received special worship from the farmers of the floating gardens of Xochimilco (Fig. 22).

Xolotl (The One of a Pair) was thought of as Quetzalcóatl's twin brother, because both personified the planet Venus, Quetzalcóatl, the morning star, and Xolotl, the evening star. The latter was therefore the god of twins, of miscarriages and of the ball-game *tlachtli*, so important to the Mexicans because the players formed a couple which symbolized for them the duality in the cosmos. Xolotl, who was represented as having the head of a dog, had many functions: among other things he helped the sun at night across the under-world stream, Chicomahuapan.

Xolotl is one of the earliest deities in Aztec mythology. Once when the sun ceased to shine and the first world age came to an end, he was the first to jump into the sacrificial fire; by this self-sacrifice he turned into the sun, which again rose in the east. The other gods followed his example. In this self-sacrifice to sustain the order of the world lies one of the reasons for the blood sacrifice which played such a large part in the life of the Mexican peoples and grew to such horrible dimensions when they were terrified by prophecies of doom just before the arrival of the Spaniards.

Yacatecuhtli (Lord of the Nose) was the tutelary god of the travellers of the merchant class. As the merchants not only traded on their long and dangerous journeys, but were also emissaries and spies of the king, they enjoyed the same respect as the warriors. Their departure and their safe arrival back were celebrated with lengthy rituals before the idols of Yacatecuhtli. He was dressed like a warrior, but held the staff of the traveller in his hand, and wore an ornament in his nose.

ILLUSTRATIONS

1. Popocatépetl Seen from Puebla Highway

The „smoking mountain" of the Aztecs is 5452 metres high, the highest but one of the snow-covered mountains in the country and yet much more easily climbed than many of the lower ones. On the north side there is a pass, the Paso de Cortés (3685 metres) which the Spaniards climbed on November 3rd, 1519, on their way to the valley of Mexico. Seventy years ago it took considerable preparations before one could venture to climb Popocatépetl as it could not possibly be done in one day. Today one can go by car from Amecameca on a fairly good road, built of coarse loamy stone and volcanic slack, up to the treeless region of Tlamacas (3925 metres). From there it is a 6 to 7 hours' climb to the lowest edge of the volcano and another hour to its highest point. Here, on a clear winter's day one gains a magnificent view of alpine, temperate and subtropical regions between the high plateau of Anáhuac and the Pic of Orizaba.

2. Mexico: View of the Cathedral

The „Zócalo", one of the largest squares of the world, was once the architectural and cultural centre of the Aztec capital Tenochtitlán. In the northeast stood the gigantic temple precinct, of far larger dimensions than the cathedral, erected on the site to eradicate all pagan memories. The main pyramid with the sanctum of the two leading deities Huitzilopochtli and Tlaloc stood on the eastern side, where the Calle de Guatemala begins, and a few remains of the temple are visible. The turquoise coloured heads of serpents which were found there had once framed the temple site and indicate a similarity to the temple of Tenayuca (fig. 34/35). Several important pieces of art were discovered under the débris such as the large calendar stone (fig. 18) and the monument of the holy war (fig. 18 and 19). Many others may still be buried under the levelling rubble.

To the east of the main temple stood the Colhuacan temple, the oldest sanctuary of Huitzilopochtli, and next to it the palace of king Axayácatl in which Moctezuma II invited Fernando Cortés and his companions on the fateful day of November 8th, 1519. The western side of the Zócalo was flanked by the palace of Moctezuma I and a „house of songs". In the southeast was situated a large group of buildings, the residence of Moctezuma II and his court. This is the site of the present National Palace. A canal run along the southern side of the precincts and a high wooden mast, a „juego de voladores" was erected there in spring, from which at the spring festivities men on long ropes swept down to the earth like birds. This game is still traditional in Papantla (Vera Cruz) and Chichicastenango (Guatemala). The present cathedral, the largest of its kind on the American

continent, was started in 1573 replacing a smaller one of 1527. It was consecrated in 1667 but not finished till 1813.

3. Mexico: Portal of the Metropolitan Chapel

This building, to the east of the cathedral, with its large dome was built between 1749 and 1768 by Lorenzo Rodriguez Lozano. The richly ornate baroque façade gives a special charm to the large block of the cathedral.

4. Mexico: The former monastery Churubusco

The monastery was originally founded by the Dominicans in the 16th century, but its present form, due to the barefooted Friars, dates from 1768. In 1847 it was used as a fortress in the war against the U.S.A. as we may see from part of the treasures on display today.

5. Mexico: The former monastery La Merced

This building in the Calle de Uruguay was originally erected between 1634 and 1703 by the Order of Divine Grace and is now used as an elementary school. It stands in the middle of a picturesque fruits and spice market. The pillared quadrangle on the first floor is probably without its equal in colonial Mexican architecture.

6. Chapultepéc,

the „grasshopper hill" was inhabited in ancient times by the Tepanecs and conquered by the Aztecs in about 1250, who founded their first modest settlement on it. Moctezuma I had an aqueduct erected to convey the wellwater from here to his capital. It was destroyed by the Spanish forces in 1520. Some of the magnificent trees in the park date back to that time.

The castle of Chapultepéc was erected in 1785 on the site of an earlier Aztec fortification. Here the unfortunate emperor Maximilian of Habsburg and his wife resided from 1864 to 1867.

7. In the Alameda Central

The word Alameda means ,poplar grove'. In Mexico many public parks have this name. The Alameda Central was laid out for the Spanish population to give them an easily accessible place for their leisure hours on the outskirts of the city. It did not always serve such peaceful purpose: many times between 1596 and 1771 the stakes of the Spanish inquisition were erected here. Today the park lies like an island in a sea of traffic. The dense foliage of the trees, which partly hide the forty-two storey skyscraper Latino-America, and the numerous fountains offer comfort even in the hottest hours of the day.

8. Mexico: Block of Houses in Multifamiliar Benito Juarez

The state is providing its civil servants with cheap yet comfortable dwellings in the form of large modern blocks of flats. Three such blocks are finished at present. Each is thirteen storeys high and consists of about a thousand flats. The estates contain shopping centres, playgrounds and sportsfields, swimming-pools, cinemas and post-offices. They are small towns within the city.

9. Mexico: The Paseo de la Reforma

is up to date the most beautiful street in the city. It leads for about 6 kilometres from the Chapultepéc-Park (fig. 6) to the city-centre. It was laid out in 1865/66 by the emperor Maximilian in imitation of the Champs Elysées in Paris and the Berlin Tiergarten. It begins as a broad avenue, surrounded by beautiful parks and repeatedly opening up into large squares with monuments, and is flanked towards the city end by impressive public buildings and skyscrapers.

10/11. Mexico: The Ministry of Transport and Labour (SCOP, Secretaría Comunicaciones y Obras Públicas)

The buildings cover an area of 93,000 square metres and consist of the government buildings of the ministry of labour and transport, where about 6000 people work every day, residential buildings for 1200 people with shops etc. on the lines of the Multifamiliares (fig. 8), a large hospital of the Seguro Social, the ministry of health and insurance. The main block has 12 storeys and consists of two long buildings standing at right angles to each other. As in the university (fig. 14/15) all free walls are decorated with mosaics in natural stone after the sketches of Juán O'Gorman.

The buildings were opened in 1954 and bear witness to the new enterprise at work in Mexico. The architects are Carlos Lazo, Raoul Cacho and Augusto Perez Palacios.

12. Mexico: Teatro Insurgentes, El Jarabe Dance

In 1955 the whole façade of the Teatro Insurgentes, situated on the large southern by-pass Avenida de los Insurgentes, was decorated with colourful mosaics by Diego Rivera and a small group of assistants. They represent cleverly blended scenes from the country's historic past in the particular, partly surrealist style of this artist: the harsh inquisition of the Spanish conquerors, the national revolution of the last century under the leadership of Hidalgo, Morelos and Benito Juarez, the social and political battles of the present and, with immediate artistic effect and seen with real love, details of Indian life in the past and in the present. Among these latter scenes is the picture of a woman dancing gracefully the traditional Jarabe on the rim of a sombrero thrown on the ground, as shown on the coloured dust-cover.

13. Mexico: Tlaloc-Fountain of Chapultepéc

An aqueduct, 62 kilometres long, carries part of the drinking water from the „Laguna de Lerma", southeast of Toluca, to the capital; its capacity is six cubicmetres per second. The walls of the well-house are decorated with frescoes by Diego Rivera who also created the double faced giant sculpture of the Aztec raingod Tlaloc symbolizing the difficult but successful struggle against the scarcity of rain.

14/15. Mexico: The University City

It was the dearest wish of the former president Miguel Alemán to transform the oldest university of the New World, founded in 1551, into one of the most modern and best equipped universities. This he succeeded in doing at an expense of more than 50 million dollars.

The university city with its colourful and boldly conceived buildings covers an area of 7.3 million square metres and was built in just over five years (the foundation stone was laid in June 5th, 1950). This feat was only made possible by the devoted cooperation of 140 architects, engineers, technicians, masons and painters under the guidance of Mario Pani and Enrique del Moral. This large settlement with its many open spaces offers housing and working space to 30,000 students and 15,000 staff.

The various buildings include: 1. The Faculty building with the Vice-Chancellor's office, the administrative offices, the professors' rooms, a library, twenty-six lecture-rooms for 1,096 students, and an auditorium for an audience of 530. 2. Scientific Institute with lecture-rooms for Geology, Astronomy, Geo-physics, Mathematics, Physics and Chemistry. 3. Economic buildings. 4. The long building of the Arts faculty. 5. Law buildings. 6. Commercial Science building. 7. The National Engineering College with low domes modelled on those of the Capilla Real in Cholula (fig. 69). 8. The National College of Architecture and Interior Decoration. 9. Institute of Nuclear Physics. 10. Institute of Radiology. 11. The huge Library block, which houses two million books and forms the cynosure of the whole university complex. The four almost windowless walls are decorated by Juan O'Gorman with mosaics in natural stone representing the Ptolemaic and Copernican eras. 12. The Schools of Medicine with a main building, laboratories, and an auditorium for 1,650 students. 13. The Chemical Institute, which has room for 1,280 students. 14. The Rectorial building, its fourteen storeys constructed entirely in glass. 15. Institute of Dental Science. 16. Institute of Veterinary Medicine. 17. The Olympic stadium for 100,000 spectators. 18. A stadium for the various branches of sport and a large swimming pool.

16. The ‚palma' of a human sacrifice

National Museum, Mexico City.

These flat ‚palmas' are fashioned in a very hard stone and decorated on both sides with a pattern of intertwined lines or human figures. They come from the Totonac region between Tajín and Jalapa. Their name derives from their shape, which resembles a palm leaf or the palm of the hand. Nobody knows quite what they were used for. Eduard Seler's thesis that they were used like the Egyptian *uschebtis* as sepulchral objects seems to be the most plausible explanation.

17. CLAY FIGURE OF A SEATED WOMAN
(From Vera Cruz. National Museum, Mexico City)
Headdress, ornaments and the contemplative attitude indicate that the small three-inch high statue was used as an idol. It resembles in style the ceramics of the third and fourth Teotihuacán period (about 800 A.D.) to which the pyramid of El Tajín belongs.

18 a. MONUMENT OF THE HOLY WAR
National Museum, Mexico City.
This monument was discovered more than a hundred years ago, but could only be extricated from its difficult position in the walls of the National Palace in 1926. It represents the model of an Aztec step-pyramid, crowned by a calendar stone, but was used as a sacrificial bowl to collect the blood of the victims. (Compare figs. 20 and 21.) In the centre the stone has a relief of the traditional sign ‚Nahui Ollin‘ (four earth movements), the date on which, according to Aztec belief, the present world will meet its doom. The sign is a kind of synonym for the sun symbol (fig. 18 b.). The stone is cut from granite and consecrated to the fifth, that is, the present sun, and to the Holy War waged in its name to gain the necessary amount of blood and hearts for its maintenance. Both sides are decorated with reliefs of gods worshipping the sun: On the obverse, Xiuhtecuhtli (Fire) and Xochipilli (Spring) with the calendar sign above them ‚One Death‘, as reproduced here.

18 b. THE LARGE CALENDAR STONE OF THE AZTECS
National Museum, Mexico City.
This stone is 3.5 metres high and weighs 24 tons. It is cut from a basalt monolith and is one of the most important documents of Aztec religion as it describes by symbols and figures the entire cosmos and its iron laws. The sun principle Tonatiuh forms its centre; on his sides hands with tiger-claws are crushing human hearts as symbols of the belief that heaven and earth on their eternal way have continually to be sustained by blood sacrifice. Round the sungod's head are inscribed the hieroglyphs of the date „Nahui Ollin" (four earth movement) frequently found on other Aztec monuments. It is indicating the date on which this world was thought to be going to disappear in an earthquake. In the corners of this part of the stone the dates of previous epochs appear: Four Tiger, Four Wind, Four Rain and Four Water. Underneath there is a fillet, inscribed with the names of the twenty days of the Old Mexican calendar: crocodile,

wind, house, lizard, snake, skull, deer, rabbit, water, dog, monkey, grass, reed, tiger, eagle, vulture, earth-movement, flint, rain and flower. As this list contains many names of animals not found in the high plateau of Mexico, such as crocodile, monkey and tiger, it is likely that the Aztecs derived their calendar system from some southern peoples, probably the Mayas.

20. DETAIL OF AN AZTEC SACRIFICIAL BOWL
National Museum, Mexico City.
The stone, though measuring 2 metres in height, is carefully worked and belongs to the best that Aztec art produced. It represents the reclining figure of the god Tlaltecuhtli. The gigantic bowl was put to the same use as the sacrificial vessel in the shape of a tiger on the opposite page.

21. RECLINING TIGER
National Museum, Mexico City.
The large statue of more than life-size with its wild head has on its back a round cavity worked in relief, a receptacle for the hearts and blood of sacrificed people.

22. THE FLOATING GARDENS OF XOCHIMILCO
with their beautiful and colourful flowerbeds form the last relics of an extensive system of lagoons in which the Aztec town Tenochtitlán lay like a kind of Venice. Their branches extend eastwards for 20 kilometres towards Mixquic-Chalco. These picturesque gardens, called ‚Chinampas‘ by the natives, were created long before the Conquest when an ever growing population needed more fertile soil. The clever Indians knew how to gain arable soil by making artificial islands along the swampy shores of the lake by sinking large baskets into the water and filling them up with humus which they renewed every time before sowing. They also planted trees on these new islands, the roots of which held the soil together. Through the slow sinking of the water-level the ‚Chinampas‘ gradually changed into dry land.

23. OLD SPANISH WATCH TOWER AT LOS REMEDIOS
One tower stands on each side of the now unused aqueduct which here spans a wide valley before entering the city centre. The spindle-like shape of the tower enabled the watchman to change the height and direction of his position in a few steps and may be part of an originally Babylonian heritage handed down to the Spaniards by way of Arabic architecture, for it has its counterparts in the minarets of Ibn-Tulûn in Cairo and in Samarra on the Tigris.

24./25. MEXICO CITY, BASILICA OF GUADALUPE
This place of pilgrimage is at all times of the year full of worshippers. It consists of the main church dominating the wide square, „La Collegiata", built in 1709, the well-chapel „El Pocito", erected between 1777 and 1791 — its cupola of blue and yellow tiles makes it one of the friendliest buildings in Mexico — and the Capilla del Cerrito on the

Tepeyac hill. This holy shrine, situated on the ruins of a former temple of the earth-goddess Coatlicue, became in 1531 the scene of a miracle. On his way to the church of Tlaltelolco the Indian Juán Diego had a vision of the Virgin Mary in a circle of light who asked him to tell bishop Juán Zumárraga to erect a church on this spot. The bishop at first would not believe him and would only consent to obey his orders if he could produce a proof from the Virgin who then proceeded to fill the poor Indio's blanket with roses. When the Indian took the roses to the bishop a beautiful picture of Mary appeared on the blanket — the afterwards so highly venerated Virgen de Guadalupe.

On December 12th, the day the picture of the Virgin is said to have appeared on the blanket, one of the biggest festivals of the country takes place. The Indians come to Guadalupe from near and far to pray, to sing and, above all, to dance their traditional native dances. Thus the cathedral of Guadalupe does more for the unification of the various Mexican tribes than all the efforts of the politicians.

26. PORTRAIT OF THE POETESS SOR JUANA INÉS DE LA CRUZ

„The tenth muse of Mexico", a name she received during her life-time, was born in 1651, the second child of a poor settler family from Spain. She is said to have been able to read and write at the age of three. After spending some time as lady-in-waiting to the vice-reine Marquesa de Mancera in the capital, she entered the convent of Saint Jerome in 1667, where she spent most of her time on literary studies. Her moral plays derive from Ovid and are a typical product of the Spanish baroque while her numerous light and easy flowing poems at times betray strong personal passion of an unfulfilled, because unrealizable love. For unknown reasons she suddenly broke short her studies and, after severe self-castigation, she gave up her literary life and devoted herself to nursing her fellow-nuns taken ill with the plague in the epidemic of 1694. She succumbed herself to the disease in 1695 and died not yet forty-four years of age.

27. MADONNA OF THE 16TH CENTURY
Museum of Christian Art, Mexico City.

This wooden statue of a madonna with flowing hair dates probably from a time soon after the Conquest. The serene looking figure on a throne-like chair and the baby in her arms have many gothic features like some of the churches of the early Spanish period as, for instance, the reticulate vault of San Augustin Acolmán or the rose-window of Yecapixtla on fig. 72.

28. MEXICO: THE PYRAMID OF CUICUILCO

This building, which today measures 123 metres in radius and 15 metres in height, and is situated on the southern border of the university quarter, surrounded by the lava of the extinct Xitle volcano, was excavated in 1923 by Byron Cummings who described it as the oldest pyramid in America. This supposition seems confirmed by research carried out in 1949 by Helmut de Terra which indicates that the ritual mound was erected in 473 B. C. The pyramid has already got the characteristic form of later buildings: it is a step pyramid tapering towards a platform and with stairs on the east-side and a ramp on the west-side.

29./31. TEMPLE PRECINCT OF TEOTIHUACÁN

The buildings of a well laid-out precinct are grouped round an axis of 1.7 kilometres so as to form the centre of a large settlement. Here, in a kind of priests' state, flourished for 500 years a civilization, opposed to wars and human sacrifice, of a creative power never again achieved in the valley of Mexico. Their ceramics, which show different stylistic phases, have an original stamp; their subtle frescoes, unfortunately now only fragments, evoke the admiration of the modern observer. This is the more amazing if one realizes that this civilization, due to the conditions of the country, belongs to a „prehistoric age" (about 300—800 A.D.) We do not know the names of the peoples who created it, nor their language or history. This settlement, which with its residential quarters covered 7.5 square kilometres, seems to have perished in a great fire, perhaps caused by enemy action: all the habitations of the priests along the so-called ‚road of the dead' show traces of fire.

The founding of Teotihuacán until recently has been linked with the Toltecs, a branch of that tribe who founded Tula (fig. 40/45). But nowadays the experts are more cautious and describe the founders as the people of Teotihucán, since more careful investigation of the remains shows no grounds for connecting them with the Toltecs. Teotihuacán had been deserted for centuries before the Aztecs settled on the shores of lake Tezcoco. As the newcomers were not themselves capable of erecting buildings such as are found in the deserted town, they did not hesitate to ascribe them to giants or gods whose abode they thought it to have been. They therefore named the place Teotihuacán „where human beings change into gods", that is, offer themselves as sacrificial victims to the gods.

The sun-pyramid, visible from a great distance on the road to Acolman, rises on a foundation of 220 by 225 metres to a height of 65 metres and is orientated to the west. Its basis, therefore, is of almost the same size as that sprung from a quite different civilization, the Cheops pyramid in Egypt, while its height is only half of that of the Egyptian pyramid, a difference caused by the step-like shape and an obtuser angle of inclination. The present profile of the sun-pyramid is no longer quite the original one, as the excavator Leopold Batres could not help doing some damage to the walls. Unlike most of the other Mexican pyramids this pyramid consists of a massive architectural block and was erected in one process and was not extended in successive calendar cycles.

32. TEOTIHUACÁN, MASKS ON THE QUETZALCÓATL TEMPLE

The frieze of the westside, tapering to a narrow top in four terraces, depicts among sea-shells ornaments the heads of two deities. One is the mask of the rain-god, the Aztec Tlaloc, whose attributes the shells are: a mask made up of geometrical patterns with the characteristic „glasses" of this deity. The other is a serpent's head showing its teeth, emerging from a circle of stylished feathers. This was the symbol of Quetzalcóatl, the plumed serpent, widely worshipped by the Aztecs who called the temple after him.

33. TENAYUCA: THE FIRE SNAKE XIUHCÓATL IN FRONT OF THE PYRAMID

One of these reptiles lies curled up in front of the temple precinct in the direction of each of the summer and winter solstices. They are to symbolize the daily way of the sun across the heaven, on which they accompany the solar deity (Xiuhtecuhtli, Huitzilopochtli). The snake has a curled horn on its head with seven prongs representing an S-shaped sign of the Mexican zodiac.

34./35. TENAYUCA: THE PYRAMID

The Spanish conquerors who passed this pyramid in 1519 called it „snakes' town" because of its frescoes; the Indian name signifies something like „walled-in square". After the Christianization it gradually relapsed into wilderness and was only rediscovered at the turn of the last century. Since 1925 excavations have brought to light one of the best preserved places of worship of Old Mexico.

The pyramid was erected by the Chichimecs, a tribe related to the Aztecs who are supposed to have settled here after the destruction of Tula (fig. 40/45) at the beginning of the 12th century and to have founded the first city. The complex was enlarged at least five times in the traditional manner at every calendar cycle, i.e. every 52 years. The various architectural phases can easily be distinguished: a small cubical basis of 31 by 12 metres was changed by the addition of several storeys into its present form of a steep terraced pyramid with a square dimension of 62 by 50 metres. It measures 19 metres in height. There are two chapels on the large platform, access to which is gained over two parallel stairways. In front of the three sides without stairs there is a sequence of coiled snakes cut in stone whose bodies are so intertwined that they form a wall.

36. THE MOUNTAIN TLALOC

near Amecameca — Milpa Alta — not to be confused with its much higher namesake behind Rio Frio, bars the valley of Mexico to the south-east. It derives its name from the Mexican rain-god, as every day towards noon big clouds drifting from the volcanoes behind it veil its summit, a sure sign of imminent rainfall.

37. THE ORIZABA MOUNTAIN

One may obtain some idea of the scale and variety of the mountains of Mexico from the fact that there are about 250 principal summits of over 3000 metres. The highest among them is the Orizaba (5700), the Citlaltépetl, ‚mountain of the stars' as the Indians call it, which is not easy to climb as the approach route is very long. It forms the eastern corner of the Central Mexican high plateau which drops here steeply towards the tropical lowlands and the gulf of the Caribean; on clear days it greets the ships from afar which enter harbour at Vera Cruz on their voyage from Cuba.

38. EXAMPLE OF EROSION NEAR OCOTOXCO

This lovely picture reveals a deep-seated evil which the Mexican government is trying to combat by all the means at its disposal: the unnecessary and fatal cutting down and burning of forests which seems to run in the Indio's blood ever since he first cut down the jungle to clear a space for his milpa, the maize field.

A thin layer of humus had formed on the volcanic ashes of the dry region east of the Tezcoco lake and its vegetation had been seriously affected in the last decades by the careless burning down of trees. The modest amount of humus was robbed of its natural protection and washed away by the heavy rainfalls of the rainy season. The whole region fell an easy victim to erosion.

In the background rises the mountain Malinche (4460 metres) which dominates the high plateau of Puebla.

39. IXTACCÍHUATL

The three-peaked mountain resembles the reclining figure of a woman shrouded in a cloth of eternal snow. This similarity has given the mountain its Indian name which is still in use today. This mountain, 5286 metres high, is the third highest in Mexico.

The photograph was taken from one of the towers of the chapel of the former Franciscan monastery of Huejotzingo, built in the 16th century.

40./45. TULA DE ALLENDE,

the legendary Tollan, is the place where Mexican history for the first time takes on a tangible shape. Aztec tradition has it, that Tollan was a flourishing Toltec town from 856 to 1168 A.D. when it was destroyed by the Chichimecs. In 977 A.D. Ce Acatl Topiltzin, Our Lord One Reed, was enthroned as the fifth of ten priest-kings. The first known historical date goes back to his reign: on a stone figure in Tula representing him is also engraved the Old Mexican date „eight flint", i.e. 980 A.D. This king seems to have ruled his small kingdom in an exemplary manner till, for reasons unknown, he set forth towards the south with some faithful companions to found a new settlement in Chichén Itzá (figs. 136/147).

Tula was conquered by the Aztecs in 1325 A.D. and, like most other pagan temples, it sank into ruin and oblivion. This process of annihilation was so rapid that Tollan, though mentioned by the last Indian historians as an important place, was thought by the Spaniards to be entirely a creation of legend and fiction. The excavations of Jorge R. Acosta, begun in 1940, have discovered the ruins near a new town Tula and thus confirmed the truthfulness of the Old Indian histories.

The main temple was completely destroyed by the Chichimecs and a pyramid of five steps of a height of about 20 metres, is all that is left to-day. This pyramid was usually supposed to be consecrated to Quetzalcóatl, but it is more likely, that it was dedicated to the deity of the morning-star which was called Tlahuizcalpantecuhtli by the Aztecs. Reliefs of great beauty on the south-side depicting above a procession of jaguars and pumas and underneath pairs of eagles and vultures holding human hearts in their claws indicate the ritual and artistic importance of the sanctuary. The thorn-like stones protruding from the walls once formed the support of a thick layer of stucco which used to encase the original façade. The roof of the destroyed temple was held up by huge porphyry figures in a rather realistic style representing Toltec warriors in their ceremonial clothes. These figures had been uprooted from their lofty position by the assailants, but the archeologists excavating the site have placed them on the eastern square in front of the pyramid.

44. Tula: Ometóchtli, the God of Pulque

Typical examples of this deity, which was at first wrongly identified as Chac Mool, one of the Maya rain-gods, can be found, together with the arrows of the eagle warriors and jaguar friezes, both in Tula and in Chichén Itzá: a fact which brings to mind the legend that Quetzalcóatl emigrated from Central Mexico to Yucatán.

The sculptures of a reclining man, drunk with pulque, have a square hollow in the middle to serve as receptacles for the drink offerings. In our picture a boy from modern Tula is absorbed in trying to reproduce the statue of the god in plaster.

45. Tula de Allende: Detail from the Frieze of the Eagle and the Jaguar on the Great Temple

The eagle soaring heavenward signifies the day, the jaguar, as antithesis, symbolizes the night. These originally Toltec symbols were later adopted by the Aztecs as, for example, the insignia of those warrior orders who built the rock temple of Malinalco (Plate 59).

46. A Flock of Sheep near Tula

A picturesque subject but revealing the same threat to the soil of Mexico as fig. 38. Sheep and shepherd are preparing the way for dangerous erosion. In spring the Indios burn all grazing land to encourage a quicker and more abundant growth of grass and not a single little tree is spared. Should it escape the fire the nibbling sheep and goats put an end to it.

47. Old Maize-Barn in Cuautla

This adobe building, three metres in height, looks like a huge urn. It is covered half-way down from the top with straw and has a kind of funnel to release any hot air arising from the storage of the sweet corn. According to recent research the maize (zea mays) belongs to the original plants of the Mexican high plateau and was introduced from there to Europe.

48. The Frailes, „Monks", near Actópan

rise like the Dolomites above the inter-American highroad about 110 kilometres from the city but are in reality the remnants of a disintegrated volcano. The tree jutting forth into the centre from the right of the picture is a pirul (schinus molle) which flourishes in the difficult condition of the Mexican high plateau.

49./51. The Pyramid of Xochicalco

As in the case of Calixtlahuaca (figs. 56/57) and Tepotzotlán a largish elevation at a strategically important place was the reason for the foundation of Xochicalco, an usual combination of a fortress-like garrison and sacred city. The Toltecs are supposed to have been the founders. They held this important fortress long after their city Tula had been overrun and destroyed by the Chichimecs about 1200 A. D. The buildings, excavated since 1935, are a kind of stadium for ball-games with a beautiful view of lake El Rodeo and a step-pyramid covering a surface of 20 by 22 metres on the highest point of the site. The excellently preserved frescoes give this pyramid a special place in Old Mexican art. They extend across the four sides of the lower platform and depict a huge coiled and hissing serpent, symbol of Quetzalcóatl, with stylized rattles on its tail. The space between the coiling body is filled with ornaments and seated persons, alternating stereotypes of a warrior in Toltec armour and a contemplating priest in ornated robes, feathered crown, jade ornaments in his ears and round his neck. On the higher platform hunting scenes, similar to those in the Dresden Codex, can be seen.

Xochicalco is situated about 10 kilometres as the crow flies south of Cuernavaca on the road of Alpuyeca-Ixtápan de la Sal. The Aztec name, ,hill of flowers', was wrongly chosen as the wavy bodies of the serpents, when only partly visible, in the rubble, were mistaken for garlands of flowers. Future excavations in this area promise to reveal further rich findings. Indications for this are the fact that early in 1962 tomb pillars (stelas) were uncovered which showed hieroglyphics and reliefs.

52./55. Indios from Central Mexico

The visitor strolling along the ruins of Mexico is especially charmed by meeting among them the descendants of the people who once erected these ritual buildings and in language and custom still seem to belong to the same age.

There are, above all, the Aztecs, Matlazincas and Toltecs, all members of the large group of the Nahua family.

The old farmer (fig. 53) from the region round Cuautla with his scanty beard and heavy eyelids seems to be a vivid affirmation of the supposition that all the Indians of America immigrated from Asia across the Behring straits. Their route is marked by archeological finds, such as the Folsom axe. This flat stone-age object, resembling the obsidian knife, is named after the place where the first one was found, Folsom in New Mexico. The remnants of early human habitation, weapons, utensils and fragments of clothing, are according to latest tests with radio-active carbon 14, between 8,000 and 14,000 years old.

Further support for the Asiatic origin of the Nahua and Maya peoples come from the Mongolian shape of their slit eyes and the Mongolian spot on their backs, which appears at birth and disappears later, and is also characteristic of the Chinese. Their black, straight and often scanty hair may perhaps also be mentioned in this context.

56. CALIXTLAHUACA: THE ROUND PYRAMID

This place with the Aztec name of „plain covered with houses" is situated about 8 kilometres northwest of Toluca on a steep slope. The large settlement, of which the Mexican archeologist José García Payón has only succeeded in unearthing a small proportion, seems to have had the same function as Xochicalco (figs. 49/51): it combined worship with guarding the main exit route to the north.

The amazingly roomy dwellings, perhaps intended for the priests, lie on a lower level than the sanctuaries, of which the round pyramid is the most important one. It measures 12 metres in height and 22 metres in diameter. The temple, like all turned and spiral things, was dedicated to Quetzalcóatl, the god of the wind. Three architectural phases are easily distinguishable. The originally modest foundation was erected by the Matlazincas, a Nahua tribe, who is also supposed to have founded Malinalco (fig. 59). The pyramid received its final shape from the Aztecs in the 15th century.

57. CALIXTLAHUACA: THE TZOMPANTLI

This Aztec word is probably best rendered by our „charnel house". It describes a modest outhouse without a roof, attached to the temples, and used to store the skulls of sacrificed people. The stylized skulls on the outer walls, as we find them here and in Chichén Itzá, which has cruciform foundations, are characteristic of this type of building.

58. LA QUEMADA

„Burned ground" is the name, derived from a neighbouring ranch, of a largish group of ruins dating from archaic times, and situated in a hilly country 50 kilometres southwest of lake Zacateca. Some scholars have mistakenly given it the name of Chicomoztóc, of those legendary seven caves, from where the Nahua tribes emigrated to the lagoons on lake Tezcoco.

As the place was easily accessible, it was fortified by high walls and like a castle could offer refuge to a large number of people. Within the enclosure there is a huge tower built of stone, which if it had the function of a pyramid, is most unusual in shape, as its walls were steep and smooth without the traditional division in steps. The dominating building of the site is the hall we can see in this picture. Its heavy pillars did not support a roof but formed a kind of patio.

59. THE ROCK TEMPLE OF MALINALCO,

situated about 12 kilometres east of Tenancingo near Toluca, rises for 100 metres above the small town of the same name. It is embedded in a narrow valley and the soil is very poor in spite of the subtropical climate. This situation suggests that a small, isolated group of Matlazinca-Indians settled here on their wanderings and founded this sanctuary, but also an Aztec chronicle mentions that the building was in progress here between 1501 and 1515 A.D.

The temple, probably dedicated to Tezcatlipoca, with all its sculptural details was hewn from solid rock — probably the most splendid example of its kind in Mexico and both in craftsmanship and artistic conception a splendid achievement. The almost circular main tower with its gaping serpent's mouth for a gate is very original in conception. Inside, in the rock, can still be seen the unfinished shapes of three eagles and a jaguar, symbols of the rising and setting sun and attributes of the warriors' order of eagles and jaguars which had its ritual centre here and at various other remote places.

60./61. THE BUILDINGS OF EL TAJÍN

A 500 kilometres long, varied and interesting drive past the oil cystern and burning methan-gas stations leads from the city to the atlantic coast and past Poza Rica into the tropical region of Papantla. This region, from which the Indians first derived the vanilla they have always favoured in their cocoa drink, contains relics of a lost and still little known civilization.

Not far from Papantla lies the buried city of El Tajín, ›place of lightning‹, which the Totonacs once carved out of virgin jungle. As in many of the other ruined towns of Mexico only parts of the numerous buildings have been excavated, above all (since 1935 by García Payón) the main pyramid on a square basis of 35 metres tapering in seven terraces to a height of 25 metres, which once was faced from top to bottom with coloured stucco. It is a representative of the so-called gulf-civilization whose heirs, not creators, were the Totonacs. Its 364 rectangular recesses, which break up the walls, distinguish it from all other pyramids in Mexico. Some have thought that these niches had some connexion with the calendar system, a niche for every day of the year; but their function was very likely only decorative. The beautifully varied scroll motive of the palaces of Mitla (fig. 101) runs along both ramps of the long flight of steps. It also decorates the palace of another group of buildings which have been given the name of Chico-(little) Tajín.

62. YUCCA TREE NEAR PACHUCOA
There are eighteen species of this liliaceous plant to be found in Mexico, both as trees and shrubs. The Yucca australis, illustrated here, with its long imbricate branches is the most magnificent of them all. Several different varieties grow in Yucatán. Its leaves supply the Yuta fibre and its flowers are pollinated by the yucca-moth (pronuba yuccasella).

63. CANDELABRA CACTUS NEAR IGUALA, IN THE SUBTROPICAL REGION
This cactus is a representative of the large family of Céreus, comprising about 300 species, and distinctive of all hot and dry regions in America. The Indians often plant it as a natural fence for their farms. The many branches springing from one root often reach a height of 8 metres. Its smaller relative is the Céreus grandiflorus, the queen of the night, so popular with European floriculturists.

64./65. SAN AUGUSTIN ACOLMAN
on the road to Teotihuacan has preserved its individual character better than any other monastic church in spite of secularization. It was founded in 1539 by the Augustine Friars as a missionary and teaching monastery and erected in over twenty years hard labour. The wide Renaissance portal with its many sculptures reminds the European visitor of 16th century castle gates. The discreetly decorated nave is furnished with good period pieces; the reticulated vaulting in the east-side is purely ornamental. The two-storey cloister, surrounding idyllic gardens, has religious symbols inset like escutcheons in the walls.

66. THE PASSION CROSS IN CUAUTITLÁN
As the cross had played an important part in their own religion as life-giving symbol the Indians did not hesitate to accept it and to adapt it to their own taste so that it received a characteristic Mexican stamp. In San Augustin Acolman the figure of Christ forms part of the wood of the cross in a strange stylization of the theme. The illustration shows a more usual treatment of the subject: the instruments of torture are arranged round the stem of the cross as in European baroque sculptures.

67. TLALMANALCO: DETAIL OF THE CAPILLA ABIERTA
The Capilla Abierta, Open Chapel, was part of the Franciscan monastery, founded in 1531. Its name derives from the fact that the church has no roof and the pillars are only connected by binding-vaults. The Indians were frightened of high, closed-in rooms and the Capilla Abierta tried to solve the problem of how to assemble them within the sacred walls of a church and yet under the open sky. Among the

rich but conventional relief decorations on pillars and vaults the archaic figure of a teaching Christ has a surprisingly inward expression.

68./69. CHOLULA: VIEW FROM THE CAPILLA REAL
The Royal Chapel from the middle of the 16th century with its nine naves and small domes over the intersections resembles a Moorish mosque. Like most of the other 360 churches in the former Toltec city it is built on the ruins of old Mexican temples. From the bell-tower one gets a view across the many domes to an old buried pyramid crowned by the pilgrims' church of Virgen de los Remedios. This pyramid is one of the largest in America; it covers a space of 160,000 square metres surpassing the Cheops pyramid of Gizeh in size. Its foundations are thought to go back to the Cuicuilco-civilization (fig. 28).

70./71. TEPOTZOTLÁN: A FORMER JESUIT MONASTERY
This monastery was founded in 1587 as novitiate seminary for the sons of Indians. A series of generous donations, the first from the distinguished chieftain Martin Maldonado, made possible the gradual enlargement and decoration of the buildings which were erected by the native craftsmen, till the expulsion of the order in 1767 put a sudden end to it all.
The whole complex comprises two churches, five chapels, one a copy of the Italian Loreto, four square „patios", many outhouses and extensive gardens. It is the largest and most magnificent site of its kind in the city. The rich domestic chapel and the intimate S. Joseph's chapel are decorative masterpieces.

72. YECAPIXTLA NEAR CUAUTLA (MORELOS), ROSE-WINDOW OVER THE CHURCH PORTAL
The large complex of buildings which offers a beautiful view of the northern ridge of mountains of the Mexican high plateau was erected by the Augustin Friars between 1541 and 1586. The choice of S. John the Baptist as patron saint was in keeping with the function of the monastery as mission station and seminary for young Indians and did not favour meditative retreat. Church and walls are heavily fortified with battlements. The rose-window over the simple renaissance portal is made up of seven round trefoils. This deliberate return to gothic styles is quite common in early Mexican church buildings.

73. TLAXCALA: PILGRIMS' CHURCH IN OCATLÁN
The picturesque Tlaxcala occupies a special position in the history of Christianity in Mexico. When the inhabitants opened the city-gates to the Spanish troops, it was here, in 1521, that the gospel was read for the first time on the American continent. The pulpit of the former Franciscan monastery bears an inscription commemorating this event. The pilgrims' church Ocatlán is situated on a hill dominating

the surrounding country-side. It was built at the beginning of the 18th century in honour of a vision of the Holy Virgin.

74. Taxco,
the Mexican Rothenburg or Carcassonne with its low, gaily roofed houses and handsome churches extends between the bare and rocky slopes along the modern car road towards Acapulco (fig. 79). Once it had been a modest place of transit for goods from the Caribean to the Pacific ocean till its inexhaustible silver-mines were discovered. José de la Borda, a simple immigrant from Spain, made his legendary fortune here and after building a palace in Cuernavaca he spent a good deal of his wealth on beautifying Taxco which to this day lives on the produce from the sale of its silver works.

75. The Humboldt-House in Taxco
This building dates from the 16th century and was probably erected by Chinese merchants who were in need of a place for the turn-over of their goods on their long way from Manila-Acapulco-Taxco-Mexico City-Vera Cruz to Europe. There is still a door-knocker in the shape of a Chinaman's head on the gate. In 1740 José de la Borda gave the house the neat and beautiful appearance which it has today.

76./77. Taxco: Façade of Santa Prisca
Between 1751 and 1758 Don José de la Borda, the uncrowned king of Taxco, had the present parish-church Santa Prisca erected on the modest foundations of a small 16th century church. The inside of Santa Prisca is exceedingly rich even in comparison with late European baroque churches: large altars rich in gold ornaments cover the walls and there are many sculptures and paintings. The façade is organized round the large oval presentation of Christ's baptism.

78. Mazatlán,
one of the main Mexican ports on the Pacific, has lately developed into a fashionable seaside resort because of its sheltered bay and tropical vegetation. A regular air-service connects it with La Paz on the Californian peninsula.

79. Acapulco: View from the Flamingo Hill to the West coast
Twenty years ago Acapulco, the „Old Asian Port" was still a dreamy fishing-village, its only visitors perhaps a few artists. Nowadays there are innumerable villas and skyscrapers which do not fit into the background and the small village has changed into the smartest resort on the Pacific coast.

80. In the Sierra Madre del Norte
The photograph was taken at El Palmito. A long metalled road of 330 kilometres runs through remote villages and connects Durango with the Pacific port Mazatlán (fig. 78).

The road, boldly cut into the rock, rises in numerous turns to a height of 3000 metres, passes many high ridges and then falls steeply towards the tropical region, the main road from Guadalajara to Mazatlán.

81. Landscape near Acapulco
This picturesque stream, lined by woody hills, runs in the subtropical region by the highroad from Mexico City to the Pacific. It marks the beginning of the long „Cañon de los Zopilotes", canyon of the vultures.

82. Dam of the Saints near Guanajato
At the beginning of the 17th century the Spaniards built a weir near the now derelict mining town of El Marfil. They made such a work of art of this practical building, that it can compete with the baroque bridges of Spain.

83. San Miguel de Allende,
founded in 1542 by the Franciscan Friar Juán de San Miguel, is easily reached by a road branching off north of Querétaro. Its hilly streets and pleasant colonial houses make it as picturesque a town as Taxco and Guanajato. There are many churches with baroque façades and a parish church looking far into the country, which was built in the last century by the native architect Don Zeferino Gutierrez in a romantic adaption of the European gothic style.

84.–88. Lake Patzcuaro
extends to a length of 20 kilometres in a mountainous countryside covered with forests. The people living on its shores still adhere to their traditions and customs, making this piece of earth one of the unspoilt beauty spots in Mexico. The Tarasco Indians live here, a tubby, agile race, speaking a language unrelated to any of the other Mexican dialects. Nowadays their ancient royal city Tzintzúntzan is a quiet little town which reminds the descendants of the glorious days when the Tarascos beat back all attacks of the Aztecs and were asked in the end to help them in their fight against Cortés. The Tarascos are shrewd traders, clever fishermen and hunters. Like the Mayas of South Mexico and Guatemala they carry their goods to market in high frameworks made of reed and fastened to their foreheads by leather straps. They hunt wild fowls with harpoon-like spears and drag the well stocked lake with large butterfly-shaped nets.
The small island of Janitzio with its open wooden huts hung with fishing nets has great charm and deserves the name of the Capri of Michoacán. Above the conical rock rises the modern monument to the fanatic priest José Maria Morelos, who lead the revolt against the Spaniards in 1810.

89. Potter in Tonalá
The great pleasure of the Tarasco Indians in different shapes and colours finds an outlet in the domestically produced lacquer-work which is appreciated in the whole country.

The potteries of Tonalá and Tlaquepaque near Guadalajara are another expression of the same stylistic elements. Man-size jars and vases are painted with colourful, stylized flowers before firing.

90./91. ZACATECAS (NORTH MEXICO): THE CATHEDRAL

The town, founded in 1548, is situated 2489 metres above sea-level among hills. The principal church, built about 1750 and made a cathedral in 1862, is a reminder of the former wealth which the neighbouring mines brought to the hard-working population.

92./93. OAXACA: CHURCH AND FORMER MONASTERY SANTO DOMINGO

The Dominicans decided in 1551 to enlarge the simple S. Paul's monastery and the work proceeded in various stages from 1572. The many chapels and splendid altars offered work to the native stucco-workers, carvers, painters, and gilders well into the 18th century. The graceful and playful treatment of large Bible subjects or themes of the order's history is probably an imitation of Puebla, perhaps of the Dominican Capilla de Rosario. Chefs d'oeuvres of Santo Domingo in Oaxaca include the lower choir whose ceiling is covered with the famous family tree of the Guzmáns, bene-factors of the order; the dome of the high choir with its many paintings and the rosary chapel painted throughout in pale, spring-like colours.

The former monastery has been desecrated by deliberate destruction as when the high altar was removed by govern-ment soldiers in 1869.

94./95. MONTE ALBÁN

The many races of the region of Oaxaca are still dominated by two tribes who differ in their way of life and language. In the eastern and southern lowlands up to Tehuantepéc live the friendly Zapotecs, in the western mountains dwell the shyer Mixtecs, the „people from the land of clouds“, who immigrated at a comparatively late date from the direction of Tlaxcala-Puebla. Shortly before the Conquest the Mix-tecs assumed the rulership of the whole region. The threaten-ing expansion of the Aztec empire under Moctezuma II unified the two tribes for a short time and though they lost Monte Albán to the Aztecs the independance of the tribes was not really diminished.

The civilization of Monte Albán, which lasted for about 1200 years, has been divided into five periods based on the different styles of the rich pottery finds. The third of these, which has some resemblance to the civilizations of Teotihua-cán and the southern Mayas, lasted the longest and was one of the most fertile. Most of the buildings which have come down to the present day probably date from it. The last period is characterized by the Mixtec culture which differs slightly from that of the Zapotecs in its deities, writing and calendar system.

Monte Albán was an old Zapotec temple town. It lies an hour's drive west of Oaxaca, bordered by mountains and built on a specially levelled hill about 1800 metres above sea-level.

The centre of the site so far discovered is a large square flan-ked by temples, a kind of Old Mexican forum. Round these buildings with their great flight of stairs and the ball-court lie hundreds of tombs of the different periods.

96. MONTE ALBÁN: CLAY URN IN TOMB 104

The two side-walls of the small tomb are decorated with frescoes which are among the best preserved of the pre-Spa-nish paintings. They depict striding men; the god of spring, Xipe Totec and the Zapotec god of agriculture, Pitao Co-zobi, in rich robes and headgear and with an incense cup for copal in his hands. He is also represented on the clay urn in the altar recess.

97. CLAY URN OF XIPE TOTEC,

from Monte Albán, now in Mexico City, National Museum. Whereas the Aztecs gave the god of the annual return of spring personal features, the Zapotecs who first worshipped this god, represented him in archaic abstract forms. The finely wrought bodily ornaments and the stylized skin of a sacrificial victim, which Xipe normally carries over his shoulder, forms a striking contrast with the stupid gnome-like expression on the tattooed face of this seated figure.

98. MONTE ALBÁN: A DANCER

The strikingly vivid reliefs, done in simple outline on lime-stone, date from the first pre-Zapotec period (about 300 B.C.). Some of them were used as building-materials for the tem-ples. It is not certain whether they depict actual ritual dan-ces. It was of particular value to research that some of these plates were inscribed with writing and numbers, probably the oldest of their type in the central American region. Close examination would seem to indicate some connection with the so-called Olmecs of La Venta (Plates 134, 135).

99. BREAST-PLATE AND MASK IN CAST GOLD

Oaxaca, Provincial Museum.

During his excavations in 1932 Alfonso Caso discovered in tomb 7, Monte Albán, a number of golden ornaments, of which this mask is one of the most carefully wrought. This beautiful work of art is rendered even more precious by its rarity for most of the other examples of goldsmith work have disappeared in the melting-pots of Europe.

The breast-plate, measuring about $9^1/_2$ centimetres, probably belonged to the nobleman buried here and is described as a god of death, the Aztec Mictlantecuhtli, whose head, in the shape of a skull, emerges from the gaping mouth of a ser-pent. The head-dress, modelled on that worn by priests, con-sists of feathers and flowers. The necklace depicts the eagle in a downward swoop, the Aztec Cuauhtemoc, a synomym for the setting sun. The ear-pendants end in snake heads. On both breast-plates are Mixtec glyphs, dates which may refer to the time they were made or consecrated: year „10 wind", „2 flint" and „11 house".

100. MITLA NEAR OAXACA, PALACE OF THE COLUMNS

Both the former Zapotec name Liobáa and the Aztec one mean something like „Place of rest", an allusion to the Aztec realm of the dead, Mictlan, for Mitla was, surprisingly enough, the realm of the living and the dead. The dead of the reigning house were buried here but the king sometimes came to live in this block-like palace which was the permanent residence of the high-priest who presided over the cult of the dead. As everywhere else in early Mexican history dates are hard to come by, but it seems to be an established fact that the whole site had existed for a very long time when the Aztecs conquered Monte Albán in 1494 A.D.

The five palaces of Mitla, one of which is now a Christian church, formed organic parts of an enormous edifice. The largest of them, the „Palacio de las Columnas" is the best preserved. Stairs lead up to low portals from the centre of a kind of forecourt. They form the only break on the massive horizontally striped façade. One longs for the false vaulting of the Mayas or any other kind of pillar which would break the monotony. The squatty columns in the first hall and also found in similar positions in other buildings create, therefore, an amazing effect.

101. MITLA: WALL IN THE PALACE OF COLUMNS

Like the peoples of Asia Minor the Mexicans may have found the meandrian pattern by watching a stream winding in and out, backwards and forwards, among the hills. The pattern occurs in many different civilizations, especially on pottery. Here it is found, as on many buildings, in the form of a „greca escalonada", a step-like broken Vitruvian scroll, which may also have some ritual significance. The pattern occurs in at least 14 variations on the outer and inner walls of the buildings in Mitla. It is formed by stone slabs on which the pattern was first chiselled at two different heights of relief to give the impression of very minutely worked mosaics. At least 100,000 stone slabs had to be worked in this way for the „Palacio de las Columnas" alone.

102. CYPRESS TREE NEAR OAXACA

Taxodium mucronatum is a species of cypress. This tree was thought to be the oldest on the American continent till remnants of the Sequoia gigantea were discovered in the Sierra Nevada. The „Sabino" of Tule is at least 2000 years old. It is 40 metres in height, the huge crown, which can be seen from a great distance, has a radius of 46 metres and the weight of the whole tree has been reckoned to be about 550,000 kilograms.

It was under a similar tree, the famous „Arbol de la Noche Triste" in Mexico-Tacuba, that Cortés on July 1st, 1520, lamented his misfortune after the disastrous retreat of his troops from Tenochtitlán.

103. INDIANS AT THE FORD AT OAXACA

Every Saturday the Indians come by foot or on horseback from their villages to the provincial market town to put their goods up for sale. All those coming from a north-western direction have to ford a river since there is no bridge.

104./105. KNEADING TORTILLAS

The nourishing flat maize cakes with their earthy flavour have formed the staple diet of the Indians in Central America for centuries, supplemented perhaps by Chile peppers, the twin to our paprika, the cloudy Agave drink pulque and the small brown bean, the „frijoles" which are boiled to a thick paste and eaten with every meal. The dough of the tortillas is first kneaded on a low stone stool with four legs, a „metate", numerous specimens of which were found among prehistoric utensils. When the dough has been reduced by a stone roller to a certain consistency the housewife takes it up and tossing it from hand to hand beats it into a thin sheet. Then it is baked on a baking plate over a moderate fire of maize straw and dished up immediately, for the tortillas have to be eaten hot.

The main ingredient of the tortillas is the Nixtamal, the name the present-day Indians give to the maize flour. Before the corn is ground or boiled it is freed from the hard husk by an addition of calcium, which is often thought to be responsible for the good condition of the teeth of Indians right up to old age.

106. ZAPOTEC WATCHMAN IN MONTE ALBÁN

The Zapotecs, a kind and shrewd race, are proud of their great cultural past and of the fact that two leading personalities came from their ranks: Benito Juarez and Porfiro Díaz. Descendants of Juarez still live in the neighbourhood of Oaxaca.

107./110. MARKET SCENES AT OAXACA

Though the provincial capital is often visited by foreigners for its good climate and the nearby ruins of Monte Albán and Mitla, the neighbouring market towns of Tlacolula, Etla, Coyotepéc and Ocatlán give a still delightfully unspoilt picture of Indian life.

108./109. MAYA CHILDREN AT SCHOOL

From the province of Chiapas. „Take the bandage from your eyes" was a recent slogan on a stamp of the National Association for the general introduction of elementary education. Attendance at school is now compulsory which should eventually abolish illiteracy.

111. Onyx Mine of La Margarita near Etla (Oaxaca)

This is the only place were the green Onyx, a marble-like hard crystal, is mined in open work. Cut in thin slabs or cubes and polished, it is in great demand in the United States. The Indians use it among other things for fashioning it into hard wearing mortars and pedestals. A brown, less valuable Onyx is mined in the neighbourhood of Puebla.

112. Woman in Tehuantepéc

The richest native dresses have been preserved in the state of Oaxaca, and are worn and shown off with pride on the many church festivals. The women's dresses of Tehuantepéc are especially colourful and varied; a working-day version of it is worn daily. It consists of a slightly flared wrap-over skirt of flowered material with a frill from hemline to waist. The blouse falls loosely over the skirt; it is a simple rectangular piece of cloth with openings for the head and the arms and stitched on the sides. While these simple everyday clothes are traditionally Indian, the rich festive dresses with their wealth of velvet and brocade trimmings and the finely pleated veils are strongly influenced by Spanish clothes. Unfortunately no research has been done as yet into this branch of Mexican folklore.

113. Maya Girls arraying themselves

Chichén Itzá. The clothes of the inhabitants of Yucatán excell in whiteness; chroniclers of the 16th century already remark on their fanatic love of cleanliness. Today the women still wear their „huipiles", white blouses with a small stole embroidered with a gay pattern.

114., 117.–125. Various Chamula Indians

Some Indian tribes, called „Chamulas" collectively, still live in the country near San Cristobal de las Casas. They speak one of the Maya dialects, Tzotzil, and are easily recognized by their characteristic clothes. The Chamulas, properly speaking, known as shrewd traders, wear a white wool poncho, leather belt and kneelength white trousers; the large straw hat has no fixed or traditional shape. The Zinacantecos (bat-men) can be identified by their red and white-striped shirt, the pink and white poncho, short white trousers and large straw hat decorated with coloured ribbons. They call themselves descendants of the Aztec warriors, even kings, but at some period in the past adopted the Maya language of their neighbours. The inhabitants of the village of Tenejapa (Over the deep Precipice) wear a black or black and white striped poncho of heavy wool, white shirt and grey shorts. Instead of these they sometimes wear a long and fringed, shawl-like poncho, and large beribboned hats.

The Huistecos differ from their neighbours in wearing a white, red-striped undergarment which resembles wide breeches, not unlike the traditional old Maya trousers still worn in Guatemala.

115. San Cristobal Las Casas: Church of Santo Domingo

This seventeenth-century church is modelled on churches of Guatemala, the neighbouring country to which the province of Chiapas belonged up to about 1875.

116. Aztec war dance, Toluca

Rhythmic dancing, culminating in a kind of frenzy, to the hollow sound of the Huehuetl drum was for the people of Old Mexico both an expression of ‚joie de vivre' and part of their ritual. Nothing much has changed in this except that nowadays the Spanish guitar and the African marimba, a kind of xylophone, are preferred to the drum. There is hardly any festival in the country which is not celebrated by dancing.

117. Chamula: The old harp player

Accompanied by a solitary guitar, he kept strumming the same pentatonic melody, resembling some ancient lullaby. When I asked him whether he could play anything else, he replied proudly. „We have had this tune in our village for as long as I can remember. We play it for weddings and funerals and we need no other."

121. Zinacantán

„The place of the bats" is situated in a sheltered position ten kilometres from S. Cristobal. Like Chamula and Tenejapa, it is a natural fortress against attacks from the north. It was a market town of importance as early as pre-conquest days. Here the Aztec merchants dealt in the precious feathers of the Quetzal (humming) bird.

124. Zinacantán: Indian plaiting a straw hat

The sombrero needed by everyone of whatever social position can be acquired at the market for very little, but it only lasts for a short time. It is a home-made article, whether the Indians require it for their own use or for sale. One can see them in front of their houses weaving the straw in their hours of leisure. They even do this work while trudging across the country, so that they measure distances and time in terms of the weaving done. If you ask an Indian how far it is to the next village, you may receive the answer, „About one-and-a-half straw hats away."

125. The straw weaver's sandals

The *huaraches* or sandals made of several layers of tough leather with a high back to protect the heels are fastened to the feet by a leather strap which passes between the big toe and its neighbour. The very same sandals are illustrated in manuscripts of the sixteenth century.

126. At the Rio Lacanjá: A Lacandone

The Lacandones are an isolated group of Mayas who live a lonely life as hunters in the forests of southern Mexico and

Guatemala. They proudly call themselves the descendants of those priest-kings who fled to the mountains after their unsuccessful attempt to defend their country against the Spaniards. Ever since those days they have refused to have anything to do with urban civilization. According to cautious estimates they number about 200 to 400 souls.

127. POTTERY IN AMANTENANGO DEL VALLE
The quiet village of Amantenango is situated on the road from San Cristobal to Comitán which one day will be one of the two main highways to Guatemala and an important extension of Panamerican Highways. The popular pots with their pretty edge patterns are only lightly fired out of doors over an open fire.

128./129. PALENQUE: THE PALACE AND TEMPLE OF INSCRIPTIONS
This place derives its unique charm from the fact that it is situated in the dense jungles of Chiapas. It is a lost city of great dimensions and superb craftsmanship, witness to a past art which flourished in the seventh and eighth century A.D. and came to an end about 1200. It is rightly compared to the French rococo style.

The town, whose lightly-built houses perished long ago, stretches for more than five kilometres on both sites of the river Otolum. Its centre is the massive palace resting on the top of a hill, and a series of pyramids, seven of which have been excavated to date. They include a ball-court similar to that of Chichén Itzá (figs. 144/145). The most important of these buildings have been carefully restored.

The palace covers a surface of 96 by 68 metres and consists of a suite of rooms opening on a court. On the northern side of the court is a stumpy tower on a square basis, the only one of its kind so far discovered in Central America. Unlike „El Caracol" of Chichén Itzá (fig. 143), the function of this tower is not known.

The Temple of Inscriptions receives its name from a long list of glyph-texts inside the building. The lower part consists of nine terraces bisected by very steep stairs.

The actual sanctuary is formed by two parallel windowless corridors, roofed over by the typical false vaulting (fig. 146). The roof has a crest-like top with an ornamental profile characteristic of Maya architecture, and forms an harmonious counterpart to the heavy mass of the building beneath. It was here that Alberto Ruz in 1952 discovered the first untouched tomb of a priest of the Maya civilization. The discovery caused great amazement as it had been assumed that only the Egyptian pyramids were used as burial vaults and that the pyramids of Central America had a mere ritual function.

130. JADE MASK FROM THE TOMB IN PALENQUE
Now in the National Museum, Mexico City.
This small piece of art covered the face of the deceased

perhaps to save it symbolically from destruction. It is strangely expressive. The mask was found in pieces and has carefully been reconstructed.

131. PALENQUE: THE TOMBSTONE IN THE TEMPLE OF INSCRIPTIONS
The tomb lay hidden in a stalactite crypt and was covered with this huge limestone slab. It depicts in relief a stylishly appareled man in a half-sitting, half-reclining attitude, probably the priest who was buried here and who had enjoyed royal honours and may have been represented here as a ‚young maize god'. Above him is the well-known ‚cross of Palenque', a stylized tree symbolizing the fertile soil and the life-giving water. The jade mask of fig. 130 covered the face of the dead man.

The date – 9.10.00.00 – engraved on the slab corresponds, according to Morley-Thompson, to our year 633 A.D.

132. STUCCO HEAD FROM THE PRIEST'S TOMB IN PALENQUE
Now in the National Museum, Mexico City.

Palenque abounds in stucco sculpture and stucco decorations on walls, etc. There are numerous sculptures and reliefs of men in high office, performing ritual acts, but this head, though probably not a portrait, is in the first rank. It depicts the narrow, thin face of a dauntless and sensitive man, who held office with spirit and prudence. As elsewhere in Maya art, the root of his aquiline nose is prolonged upwards to the edge of his helmet-like headgear.

133. PORTRAIT: HEAD OF THE SUN GOD,
in the National Museum, Mexico City, taken from a clay cylinder about 80 cm in height. The mask comes from Palenque. A fascinating effect is achieved by very scanty ornamental means. The deity depicted here, a counterpart of the Aztec Tonatiuh, was called by the Mayas Kinich Ahau (‚Lord of the Sun's Eye').

134./135. THE GIANT HEAD AND KING'S MONUMENT FROM LA VENTA
Due to the initiative of the museum director, Carlos Pellicer, about 30 large statues were erected in a park near the airport of Villahermosa (Tabasco). These had been excavated by the North American archeologist, Matthew W. Stirling, in 1940 from the swampy area of La Venta. Whereas previously these objects were relatively inaccessible, today they are able to recall the atmosphere of a long submerged culture which once flourished in three places on the southern Gulf of Mexico. In the absence of a more exact designation, this culture has been connected with the legendary people of the Olmecs, the people from the rubber country, as the Aztecs named one of their neighbouring tribes from the south-east.

The massive heads from La Venta, with their obviously negroid features, stood detached, without torso, in the countryside and probably served to glorify some famous chiefs. These, and the square tomb stones of the same area, attain weights of more than 20 tons. Their size, and the mysterious power which these works of art radiate, give ample evidence that here a culture flourished which was the equal of that of the Mayas and which probably influenced the Mayas in many respects.

136./137. CHICHÉN ITZÁ: THE MAIN PYRAMID ,EL CASTLLLO‘

Not so long ago archeologists used to complain about the difficult road from Mérida to southern Yucatán. You can travel there now in modern buses. The drive takes three hours and the plantations of *Agave sisalana* thin out along the road till suddenly the strange outlines of the temples and pyramids appear. The name of this large and noble town, which means, roughly translated ,at the edge of the pond where the Itzas live‘ explains its probable origin. The ,pond‘ refers to the cisterns which still exist in the barren, chalky soil, the Cenotes, which became famous when Edward Herbert Thompson by repeated diving brought up numerous ritual offerings mentioned in the religious writings of the Mayas. The town was flourishing at the time when in England the period of Norman art was on the wane. It was deserted by its inhabitants for reasons unknown long before the Aztecs invaded the high plateau of Anáhuac. The ancient buildings extend for miles right to the edge of the gloomy jungle. Seen from the road, the pyramid of Quetzalcóatl-Kukulkan, called ,El Castillo‘ by the Spaniards, dominates the town. It is a monument in honour not only of the ,white god‘ but also of the Toltec migration from Tula (figs. 40/45) to the south. The pyramid rests on an older substructure. It has nine huge terraces and is built in the shape of an Aztec Teocalli, one of those large temples the top platform of which was used for ritual sacrifice — though this was less often practised by the Mayas than the Aztecs. Each of the four stairs has 91 steps, which, together with the top platform make up the number 365, one for each day of the calendar.

138.–140. CHICHÉN ITZÁ: THE TEMPLE OF WARRIORS

The temple is named by the reliefs on the about 600 pillars which depict warriors, eagles and jaguars, with which we may compare the temple of the morning star in fig. 43. These reliefs seem to indicate that the temple was dedicated to the gods of war and to the order of the jaguar and eagle warriors. The temple rises in a harmonious line in four terraces, divided by only one stair, to a broad platform with the sanctuary. This consists of two, now roofless, halls with two lines of columns. Two more columns in the shape of coiling snakes with their heads to the ground and holding up the roof beams with their tails form the entrance to the temple. Stylistic elements of Maya and Toltec art are mixed in the decorations of the outer walls.

Underneath the temple of the Warriors is an older one of more modest dimensions, which can now be reached by a stair. The columns of this substructure, which were not exposed to sun and rain, have retained the rich original colours of their reliefs. The walls are covered with minute paintings describing the conquest of a Maya village by the Toltecs.

141. CHICHÉN ITZÁ: STANDARD BEARER ON THE RAMP OF THE TEMPLE OF WARRIORS

There is a figure of a seated man above a serpent's head on both sides of the top of the staircase. He holds in his hands a hollowed stone in which a standard of feathers was stuck on festive days.

142. CHICHÉN ITZÁ: ,EL MERCADO‘

The tall slender columns which form the forecourt of the long-drawnout building have given rise to the supposition that this was once a market.

143. CHICHÉN ITZÁ: ,EL CARACOL‘

,El Caracol‘ is nowadays, after many alterations, a round tower, 16 metres in height, on a rectangular, but not a square basis such as we find in Palenque (fig. 128), with a helmet-like dome. It derives its Spanish name from the remnants of a spiral staircase, which leads to a room on the top floor. The window recesses of this modest room were used by the priests of Quetzalcóatl-Kukulkan when they gave out the times when day and night were of equal length and the periods when the sun ceased to move. Standing in a corner diagonally opposite to the outer edge of the opening in the outer wall, they took the measurements of the horizon.

144./145. CHICHÉN ITZÁ: THE BALL-COURT

The game ,Tlachtli‘, which was very popular with many Indian tribes in Central America, and is still played occasionally, required a great deal of energy and skill in the two partners or teams competing. The hard rubber ball had to be driven across the long narrow court by agile movements of the body without using the arms or legs and then struck with the hip through a stone ring fixed at the height of about three metres at both ends of the court.

As we may see from limestone sculptures of the Tarasco Indians and from fragments of a frescoe at Tepantitla, other ball games involving the use of wooden sticks as in European hockey were popular, but their rules were probably different from those of ,Tlachtli‘. Though this game was useful for strengthening and improving physical fitness and was popular as an interesting spectacle for large crowds, its chief significance was as ritual. The court, which is said to include the calendar sign ,Ollin‘ (fig. 18), represented the cosmos, in which the play of the natural powers gives victory to this or that side, and the ball also signified the course of the planets across the heavens.

Almost all the known temple sites included a ball-court of this type, some with vertical, others with convex walls. The ball-court of Chichén Itzá is architecturally outstanding in that it includes the Temple of the Warriors in the design. The well-preserved stone rings have retained the usual relief decoration of braided serpents.

146. Two examples of a Maya vaulting
The oldest constructions of this kind are the sepulchral vaults in the lost town of Uaxactún in the jungles of Guatemala, dating from the fourth century A.D. In spite of their inherent limitations, they were retained during all the Maya civilizations. The false vaulting is formed by two parallel walls, in which, about half-way up, wedge-shaped stones gradually converge until they touch or are joined by a covering stone at the top. This method of vaulting is found in different civilizations all over the world (as in Mykene, Angkor Vat, Konarak in India).
Fig. 146b shows the entrance to the Temple of Inscriptions. An especially fine example is found at Labnah near Kabah (fig. 146). It is a decorated gate resembling an ,Arc de Triomphe' and stands by itself.

147. Chichén Itzá: „las Monjas"
As in Uxmal (fig. 150) the Spaniards thought this was a nunnery governed by priestesses and gave it the name ,Las Monjas'. This massive building measuring 70 by 35 metres is a remarkable example of the fretted ornamentation of the pre-Toltec ,Puuc' style.

148. Uxmal: House of the Tortoises
This building at the north-east side of the huge platform of the Governor's palace derives its name from a frieze of tortoises running along a string-course in the cornice. Nothing is known of the purposes served by this example of classic simplicity. The inhabitants of the neighbouring villages believe that its priests practised the art of weather-making, since whenever tortoises appear in numbers, they are a sure sign of rain after a dry period.

149. Uxmal: The Governor's Palace
The town of Uxmal received its final form under the Xiu princes who reigned in the years 1000—1200 A.D. The des-

cendants of this family survive as simple peasants in Ticul. Uxmal is on the site of an older Maya town, a fact which has puzzled archeologists because there are no wells there, whereas Chichén Itzá had three. Perhaps the water supply came from the abundant rains. During the period mentioned above, Uxmal was probably one of the largest and most important Maya towns of Yucatán.
The Casa del Gobernador or Governor's Palace is 98 metres long and only 12 metres wide. It is divided longitudinally by a wall into two narrow corridors. These two areas are lighted by narrow slits in the walls and have each one entrance only on the side of the façade. The two ornamented fronts of similar composition are connected only by two corridors at the back. Above a plain wall runs a frieze consisting of scroll-like geometrical patterns and masks of the rain gods.

150. Uxmal: ,Las Monjas'
This imposing building forms a rectangle 50 metres by 75 metres and its 88 rooms open only on the inner court. It obtained the name of nunnery from the belief that women were here trained to become priestesses. The ornamentation on the four outer walls is so rich and complicated that it is difficult to describe in detail.

151. Kabah
lies 95 km on the present-day highway from Mérida to Campeche. It marks the end of the creative period of the golden age in architecture of the Maya towns of Yucatán (*about* 1100 A.D.). The magnificent façade of the temple Codz Poop (,First House') is decorated with masks of the rain god Chac in a series of geometric shapes with trunks projecting at regular intervals from the façade.

152. A Ranch near Tapachula in the province of Chiapas.
A few kilometres away lie the river Tacaná and the occasionally active volcano of the same name, which forms the natural frontier between Mexico and Guatemala. On the slopes of this volcano, which reaches a height of 4200 metres, are grown the most valuable varieties of coffee produced in this tropical region.

LIST OF THE PLATES

6

16

24

49

73

85

93

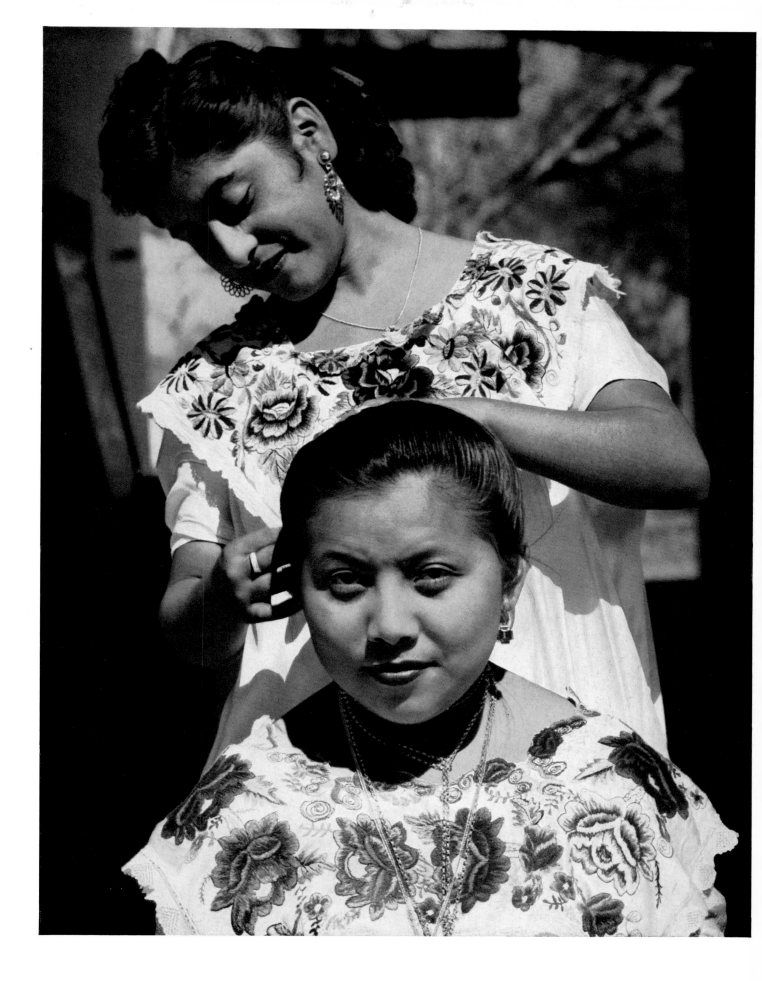

119

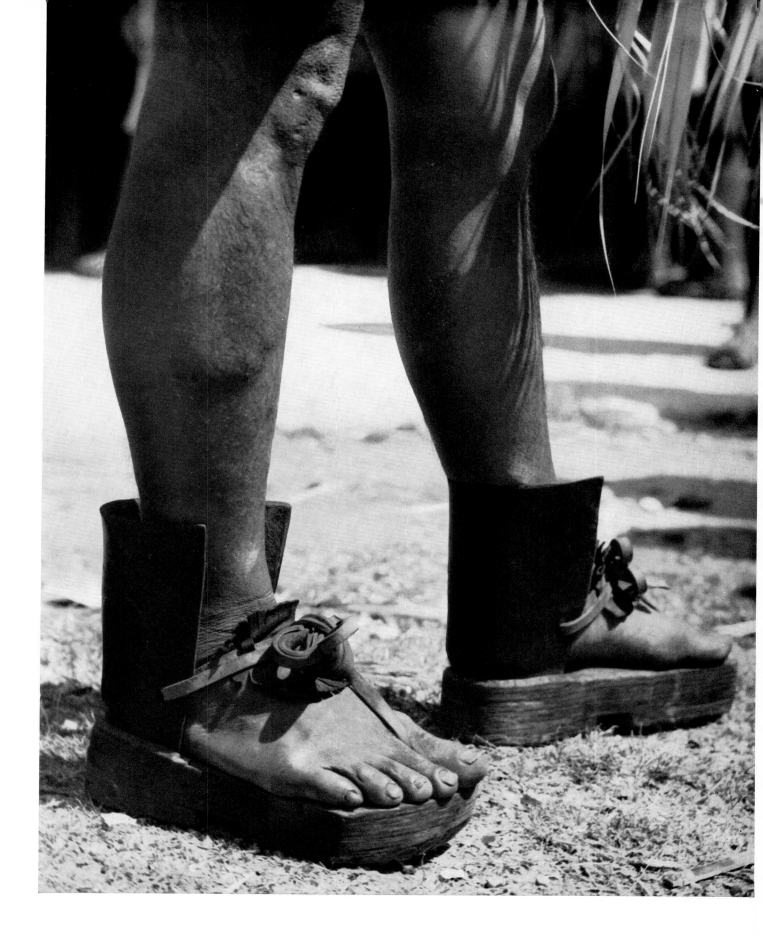

138

149